the final foucault

edited by
james bernauer and david rasmussen

The MIT Press
Cambridge, Massachusetts
London, England

This work originally appeared as volume 12, nos. 2–3, of the journal *Philosophy and Social Criticism*.

This book was printed and bound in the United States of America.

Library of Congress Cataloging-in-Publication Data

The Final Foucault.

1. Foucault, Michel.   I. Bernauer, James William.
II. Rasmussen, David M.
B2430.F724F56   1988   194   87-36656
ISBN 0-262-52132-6 (pbk.)

This book is in a special program to extend the life of significant MIT Press titles. It has been produced using an on-demand printing process that allows the publisher to print books in relatively small quantities. Because of the nature of the process, printing quality may be slightly compromised in comparison to the original printing.

table of contents

an introductory note

When Michel Foucault died in June, 1984, French bookstores had just received two long-awaited studies in his project of a history of sexuality. It had been eight years since the publication of the initial volume in this series. Even a rapid inspection of these new books made it immediately evident that this period of reflection had sheltered novel departures for a philosophical project which had not yet been adequately absorbed. **The Use of Pleasure** and **The Care of the Self** treated Greek and Roman ethics, a new field of research for Foucault. For most of his readers, these works were as unexpected as his death. Both reiterated the personal style he proclaimed in 1969, when he replied to the criticism that he was always shifting his interests and positions: "I am no doubt not the only one who writes in order to have no face. Do not ask who I am and do not ask me to remain the same: leave it to our bureaucrats and our police to see that our papers are in order. At least spare us their morality when we write."[1] The statement is vintage Foucault: an experience of thinking that is identified with an art of escaping the demands of what others consider thought-worthy; a sense of the danger posed to intellectual life by any subordination to a professional bureaucracy or even to one's own professed project; and, finally, a personal pleasure in being different, in not appearing with the face his commentators predicted on the basis of earlier writings. As Foucault once put it: "No, no, I'm not where you are lying in wait for me, but over here, laughing at you."[2] Despite that laugh, which was so distinctive of the man, death has forced upon his project a definitiveness which allows us to give his work a face, not a death mask but a clear shape inviting further recognition and exchange. Shortly after Foucault's death, we planned this special issue of **Philosophy and Social Criticism** as a tribute to his new works and as a critical comprehension of the culminating stage in Foucault's thought which they represented.

While care of the self became the title of only one of Foucault's books, it was his concern with the self, and with the problematics swirling around it, that provided the major themes for his thought from 1976 to 1984. We are privileged to include as part of this issue an important discussion which Foucault had just five months before he died. We are very grateful to the editors of **Concordia** for permission to publish it here in its first English translation.[3] This interview is one of Foucault's clearest statements about the horizon within which he put his approach to ancient culture and why he regarded it as the best formulation of his entire project. The various motifs which Foucault stressed in this discussion are developed in the series of essays which follow it here. In his "Michel Foucault, Rameau's Nephew, and the Question of Identity," Karlis Racevskis directly confronts the issue of identity which surfaces so frequently in Foucault's writings. Racevskis shows how Foucault's critique of culture leads to his ultimate task of redefining the self's relation to the self, of getting away from the self. Foucault described this task as central to the motivation for his last investigations: "As for what motivated me, it is quite simple; I would hope that in the eyes of some people it might be sufficient in itself. It was curiosity—the only kind of curiosity in any case, that is worth acting upon with a degree of obstinacy: not the curiosity that seeks to assimilate what it is proper for one to know, but that which enables one to get free of oneself. After all, what would be the value of the passion for knowledge if it resulted only in a certain amount of knowledgeableness and not, in one way or another and to the extent possible, in the knower's straying afield of himself?"[4]

This straying afield of himself brought him to a more explicit relationship to the work of philosophy which the interview describes as a particularly intense form of care of the self: "in degree of zeal for self—and hence in zeal for others as well—the position of the philosophy is not that of any free man." Garth Gillan's "Foucault's Philosophy" examines his last theoretical desires and their new role in his design to engage philosophy as thought of the other. Gillan's essay indicates how Foucault shifted from a study of our culture's will to know to the discovery of an erotics of knowledge which functions as the prelude to a new style of philosophizing. James Bernauer's "Michel Foucault's Ecstatic Thinking" emphasizes the ethical commitment of that philosophizing and uncovers the mode of thinking which animates it. This essay also presents a context for Foucault's last questions by sketching his scrutiny of Christian experience, which would have become part of the announced fourth volume in the history of sexuality: **Confessions of the Flesh**. Although this volume will not appear, its investigations were chronologically prior to Foucault's consideration of ancient culture and strongly influenced that later inquiry. Foucault's final writings carry forward his philosophical history of the truth, and it is this advance which is the focal point of our other two contributors. Diane Rubenstein's "Food for Thought: Metonymy in the Late Foucault" proposes a Lacanian interpretation of Foucault's last works by reading their linkage of desire, power and truth in terms of a coherent strategy of metonymy. The significant change exhibited in late Foucault is a rhetorical displacement, a displacement which illuminates both his theory of desire and his struggle with truth. Thomas Flynn's "Foucault as Parrhesiast: His Last Course at the Collège de France" gives an account of Foucault's last lectures, for which Flynn himself was present. The theme of those lectures was the practice of truth-telling as a moral virtue in the ancient world. Flynn perceives the course as a kind of "homecoming" for Foucault's abiding interest in the history of truth.

The continuing interest which that history will hold for Foucault's future readers should be served by the complete bibliography of Foucault's works on which James Bernauer and Thomas Keenan have worked for several years. It will be this distinguished body of writings which will be the lasting identity of Michel Foucault, whose historical chronology closes our issue.

James Bernauer
David Rasmussen

NOTES

1. **The Archaeology of Knowledge**, trans. by A. M. Sheridan Smith (New York: Harper Colophon, 1976), p. 17.

2. **Ibid**.

3. The interview was conducted by Raúl Fornet-Betancourt, Helmut Becker and Alfredo Gomez-Müller on January 20, 1984, and published in **Concordia: Internationale Zeitschrift für Philosophie** 6 (1984), pp. 99–116.

4. **The Use of Pleasure**, trans. by Robert Hurley (New York: Pantheon Books, 1985), p. 8.

the ethic of care for the self as a practice of freedom

an interview with michel foucault on January 20, 1984

conducted by raúl fornet-betancourt, helmut becker, alfredo gomez-müller

translated by j. d. gauthier, s.j.

Q: First of all, we would like to know what is the object of your thought at this moment. We have followed your recent development, especially in your courses at the Collège de France (1981–1982) on the hermeneutic of the subject. We would like to know if your present philosophical research is still determined by the poles, subjectivity and truth.

MF: In fact, that has always been my problem, even if I have expressed in different terms the framework of this thought. I have tried to discover how the human subject entered into **games of truth**, whether they be games of truth which take on the form of science or which refer to a scientific model, or games of truth like those that can be found in institutions or practices of control. That is the theme of my book **The Order of Things**, where I've tried to see how, in scientific creation, the human subject will be defined as an individual who talks, who works, who lives. It is in my courses at the Collège de France that I tried to outline this problem in its generality.

Q: Is there not a "leap" between your previous thought on this problem and that of subjectivity/truth and specifically beginning with the concept of care for self?

MF: Up to that point, the problem of the relationship between the subject and the games of truth had been faced in two ways: either beginning with coercive practices—(as in the case of psychiatry and the penitentiary system)—or in forms of theoretical or scientific games, as for example, the analysis of the riches of language and of the living being. Now, in my courses at the Collège de France, I try to grasp the problems through what one might call a practice of the self, a phenomenon which I believe to be very important in our societies since Greek and Roman times, even though it has hardly been studied. In Greek and Roman civilizations these practices of the self had a much greater importance and autonomy than later on, when they were laid siege to, up to a certain point, by institutions: religious, pedagogical, or of the medical and psychiatric kind.

Q: There is now a sort of shift: these games of truth no longer are concerned with coercive practices but with the practices of self-formation of the subject.

MF: That is correct. It is what one might call an ascetical practice, giving the word "ascetical" a very general meaning, that is to say, not in the sense of abnegation but that of an exercise of self upon self by which one tries to work out, to transform one's self and to attain a certain mode of being. I am taking the word "asceticism" in a wider sense than Max Weber, but it is much along the same line.

Q: A work of self upon self which can be understood as a kind of liberation, as a mode of liberation?

MF: I shall be a little more cautious about that. I've always been a little distrustful of the general theme of liberation, to the extent, that, if one does not treat it with a certain number of safeguards and within certain limits, there is the danger that it will refer back to the idea that there does exist a nature or a human foundation which, as a result of a certain number of historical, social or economic processes, found itself concealed, alienated or imprisoned in and by some repressive mechanism. In that hypothesis it would suffice to unloosen these repressive locks so that man can be reconciled with himself, once again find his nature or renew contact with his roots and restore a full and positive relationship with himself. I don't think that is a theme which can be admitted without rigorous examination. I do not mean to say that liberation or such and such a form of liberation does not exist. When a colonial people tries to free itself of its colonizer, that is truly michel foucault an act of liberation, in the strict sense of the word. But as we also know, that in this extremely precise example, this act of liberation is not sufficient to establish the practices of liberty that later on will be necessary for this people, this society and these individuals to decide upon receivable and acceptable forms of their existence or political society. That is why I insist on the practices of freedom rather than on the processes which indeed have their place, but which by themselves, do not seem to me to be able to decide all the practical forms of liberty. I encountered that exact same problem in dealing with sexuality: does the expression "let us liberate our sexuality" have a meaning? Isn't the problem rather to try to decide the practices of freedom through which we could determine what is sexual pleasure and what are our erotic, loving, passionate relationships with others? It seems to me that to use this ethical problem of the definition of practices of freedom is more important than the affirmation (and repetitious, at that) that sexuality or desire must be set free.

Q: Do not the practices of liberty require a certain degree of liberation?

MF: Yes, absolutely. That is where the idea of domination must be introduced. The analyses I have been trying to make have to do essentially with the relationships of power. I understand by that something other than the states of domination. The relationships of power have an extremely wide extension in human relations. There is a whole network of relationships of power, which can operate between individuals, in the bosom of the family, in an educational relationship, in the political body, etc. This analysis of relations of power constitutes a very complex field; it sometimes meets what we can call facts or states of domination, in which the relations of power, instead of being variable and allowing different partners a strategy which alters them, find themselves firmly set and congealed. When an individual or a social group manages to block a field of relations of power, to render them impassive and invariable and to prevent all reversibility of movement— by means of instruments which can be economic as well as political or military—we are facing what can be called a state of domination. It is certain that in such a state the practice of liberty does not exist or exists only unilaterally or is extremely confined and limited. I agree with you that liberation is sometimes the political or historical condition for a practice of liberty. Take for example sexuality. It is certain that a number of liberations regarding the power of the male were needed, that it was necessary to free one's self from an oppressive morality which concerns heterosexuality as well as homosexuality. This liberation does not manifest a contented being, replete with a

3

sexuality wherein the subject would have attained a complete and satisfying relationship. Liberation opens up new relationships of power, which have to be controlled by practices of liberty.

Q: Could not liberation itself be a modality or a form of a practice of liberty?

MF: Yes, in a certain number of cases. You have cases where in fact liberation and the struggle for liberation is indispensable for the practice of liberty. As for sexuality, for example—I say this without a desire for controversy because I don't like polemics; for the most part, I think they are counterproductive—there was the Reichean model which was derived from a particular reading of Freud. It supposed the problem to be entirely in the order of liberation. To say the things somewhat schematically, there would be desire, pulsation, taboos, repression and interiorization. It is in lifting these taboos, i.e. in liberating one's self, that the problem would be solved. And there, I think that we are completely missing the moral problem—(and I know that here I am caricaturizing some very fine and interesting points of view of various authors)—the moral problem, I say, which is the practice of liberty. How can one practice freedom? In the order of sexuality, is it obvious that in liberating one's desires one will know how to behave ethically in pleasurable relationships with others?

Q: You say that liberty must be practiced ethically?

MF: Yes, for what is morality, if not the practice of liberty, the deliberate practice of liberty?

Q: That means that you consider liberty as a reality already ethical in itself?

MF: Liberty is the ontological condition of ethics. But ethics is the deliberate form assumed by liberty.

Q: Is ethics then the result of the search or care for self?

MF: The care for self was in the greco-roman world the manner in which individual liberty—and civic liberty, up to a certain point—considered itself as ethical. If you take a whole series of texts going from the first Platonic dialogue up to the major texts of the later Stoics—Epictetus, Marcus-Aurelius, etc.—you would see that the theme of **care for the self** has truly permeated all ethical thought. On the other hand, it seems that in our societies, beginning at a certain moment in time—and it is difficult to say when that happened—the care for self became something somewhat suspect. Caring for self was, at a certain moment, gladly denounced as being a kind of self-love, a kind of egoism or individual interest in contradiction to

4

the care one must show others or to the necessary sacrifice of the self. All that happened during the Christian era, but I would not say that it is exclusively due to Christianity. The situation is much more complex because, in Christianity, achieving salvation is also a caring for self. But in Christianity, salvation is obtained by renunciation of self. There is a paradox of care for self in Christianity, but that is another question. Returning to the question you were asking, I think that both with the Greeks and the Romans—and especially with the Greeks—in order to behave properly, in order to practice freedom properly, it was necessary to care for self, both in order to know one's self—and there is the familiar *gnothi seauton*—and to improve one's self, to surpass one's self, to master the appetites that risk engulfing you. Individual liberty was very important to the Greeks— notwithstanding the platitude more or less derived from Hegel, according to which the liberty of the individual would have no importance when faced with the noble totality of the city—not to be a slave (of another city, of those who surround you, of those who govern you, of one's own passions) was an absolutely fundamental theme: the concern for liberty was a basic and constant problem, during eight centuries of ancient culture. We have there an entire ethics which turned about the care for the self and which gave ancient ethics its very particular form. I am not saying that ethics is the care for self, but that in Antiquity, ethics, as a deliberate practice of liberty has turned about this basic imperative: "Care for yourself."

Q: An imperative that involves the assimilation of *logoi*, truths?

MF: Naturally. One cannot care for self without knowledge. The care for self is of course knowledge of self—that is the Socratic-Platonic aspect— but it is also the knowledge of a certain number of rules of conduct or of principles which are at the same time truths and regulations. To care for self is to fit one's self out with these truths. That is where ethics is linked to the game of truth.

Q: You say that it is a question of making this truth which is learned, memorized, progressively put into action, a sort of quasi-subject which reigns supremely in you. What is the status of this quasi-subject?

MF: In the Platonic current, at least according to the end of the **Alcibiades**, the problem for the subject or for the individual soul is to turn its gaze on itself in order to recognize itself in what it is and recognizing itself in what it is, to recall the truths to which it is related and on which it could have reflected. On the other hand, in the current that one can call globally Stoic, the problem is to learn by the teaching of a certain number of

5

truths, of doctrines, some of which are fundamental principles and others rules of conduct. It is a question of having these principles tell you in each situation, and in some way spontaneously, how you should behave. It is here that we find a metaphor that does not come from the Stoics but from Plutarch. "You must have learned principles so firmly that when your desires, your appetites or your fears awaken like barking dogs, the *logos* will speak with the voice of a master who silences the dogs by a single command." You have there the idea of a *logos* who would operate in some way without your doing anything. You will have become the *logos* or the *logos* will have become you.

Q: We'd like to return to the question of the relationship between freedom and ethics. When you say that ethics is the deliberate part of freedom, does that mean that freedom can be aware of itself as an ethical practice? Is it at the very first and always a moralizing freedom, so to speak, or must there be work on one's self in order to discover this ethical dimension of liberty?

MF: The Greeks, in fact, considered this freedom as a problem and the freedom of the individual as an ethical problem. But ethical in the sense that Greeks could understand. *Ethos* was the deportment and the way to behave. It was the subject's mode of being and a certain manner of acting visible to others. One's *ethos* was seen by his dress, by his bearing, by his gait, by the poise with which he reacts to events, etc. For them, that is the concrete expression of liberty. That is the way they "problematized" their freedom. The man who has a good *ethos*, who can be admitted and held up as an example, he is a person who practices freedom in a certain manner. I do not think that a conversion is necessary so that freedom be reflected as an *ethos* that is good, beautiful, honorable, worthy and which can serve as an example, there is need of labor of self on self.

Q: And that is where you situate the analysis of power?

MF: I think that in the measure liberty signifies for the Greeks non- slavery—a definition which is quite different from ours—the problem is already entirely political. It is political in the measure that non-slavery with respect to others is a condition: a slave has no ethics. Liberty is then in itself political. And then, it has a political model, in the measure where being free means not being a slave to one's self and to one's appetites, which supposes that one establishes over one's self a certain relation of domination, of mastery, which was called *arche*—power, authority.

6

michel foucault

Q: The care for self, you said, is in a certain fashion the care for others. The care for self is in this sense also always ethical. It is ethical in itself.

MF: For the Greeks it is not because it is care for others that it is ethical. Care for self is ethical in itself, but it implies complex relations with others, in the measure where this *ethos* of freedom is also a way of caring for others. That is why it is important for a free man, who behaves correctly, to know how to govern his wife, his children and his home. There, too, is the art of governing. *Ethos* implies also a relation with others to the extent that care for self renders one competent to occupy a place in the city, in the community or in interindividual relationships which are proper—whether it be to exercise a magistracy or to have friendly relationships. And the care for self implies also a relationship to the other to the extent that, in order to really care for self, one must listen to the teachings of a master. One needs a guide, a counsellor, a friend— someone who will tell you the truth. Thus, the problem of relationship with others is present all along this development of care for self.

Q: The care for self always aims at the good for others. It aims at a good administering of the area of power which is present in all relationships, i.e., it tends to administer it in the sense of non-domination. In this context, what can be the role of the philosopher, of the one who cares for the care of others?

MF: Let us take for example Socrates. He is the one who hails people in the street or young boys in the gymnasium, by saying to them: Are you concerned with yourself? A god has charged him with that. That is his mission and he will not abandon it, even at the moment when he is threatened by death. He is truly the man who cares for others. That is the particular position of the philosopher. But let us say it simply: in the case of the free man, I think that the assumption of all this morality was that the one who cared for himself correctly found himself, by that very fact, in a measure to behave correctly in relationship to others and for others. A city in which everyone would be correctly concerned for self would be a city that would be doing well, and it would find therein the ethical principle of its stability. But I don't think that one can say that the Greek who cares for himself should first of all care for others. This theme will not come into play, it seems to me, until later. One must not have the care for others precede the care for self. The care for self takes moral precedence in the measure that the relationship to self takes ontological precedence.

Q: Can the care for self, which possesses a positive ethical sense, be understood as a sort of conversion of power?

7

MF: A conversion, yes. It is in fact a way of controlling and limiting. For, if it is true that slavery is the big risk to which Greek liberty is opposed, there is also another danger, which appears at first glance as the opposite of slavery: the abuse of power. In the abuse of power, one goes beyond what is legitimately the exercise of power and one imposes on others one's whims, one's appetites, one's desires. There we see the image of the tyrant or simply of the powerful and wealthy man who takes advantage of his power and his wealth to misuse others, to impose on them undue power. But one sees—at least that is what the Greek philosophers say—that this man is in reality a slave to his appetites. And the good ruler is precisely the one who exercises his power correctly, i.e., by exercising at the same time his power on himself. And it is the power over self which will regulate the power over others.

Q: Does not the care for self, released from the care for others, run the risk of "absolutizing itself"? Could not this "absolutization" of care for self become a kind of exercise of power on others, in the sense of domination of the other?

MF: No, because the risk of dominating others and exercising over them a tyrannical power only comes from the fact that one did not care for one's self and that one has become a slave to his desires. But if you care for yourself correctly, i.e., if you know ontologically what you are, if you also know of what you are capable, if you know what it means for you to be a citizen in a city, to be the head of a household in an *oikos*, if you know what things you must fear and those that you should not fear, if you know what is suitable to hope for and what are the things on the contrary which should be completely indifferent for you, if you know, finally that you should not fear death, well, then, you cannot abuse your power over others. There is therefore no danger. This idea will appear much later, when love of self will become suspect and will be seen as one of the possible roots of diverse moral faults. In this new context, the care for self will have as its primary form, the renunciation of the self. You discover this in a fairly clear fashion in the **Treatise on Virginity** of Gregory of Nyssa, where you find the notion of care for self "*epimeleia heauton*" defined essentially as renunciation of all worldly attachments. It is the renunciation of all that could be love of self, attachment to a worldly self. But I believe that in Greek and Roman thought the care for self cannot in itself tend to this exaggerated love of self which would, in time, come to neglect others or worse still, abuse the power that one can have over them.

Q: Then it is a care for self which, thinking of itself, thinks of others?

MF: Yes, absolutely. The one who cares for self, to the point of knowing exactly what are his duties as head of a household, as husband or father, will find that he has relationships with his wife and children which are as they should be.

Q: But does not the human condition, in the sense of its finiteness, play there a very important role? You have spoken of death. If you are not afraid of death, you cannot abuse your power over others. It seems to us this problem of finiteness is very important: fear of death, fear of finiteness, of being hurt: all these are at the heart of care for self.

MF: Of course. And that is where Christianity, in introducing salvation as salvation beyond this life, will somehow unbalance or at least upset the whole theme of care for self. Although— and I recall it once more—seeking one's salvation will be precisely renunciation. With the Greeks and the Romans, on the other hand, beginning from the fact that one cares for self in his own life and that the reputation which we will have left behind is the only after-death with which we preoccupy our- selves—care for self can then be entirely centered on one's self, on what one does, on the place one occupies among others. It can be totally centered on the acceptance of death— which will be most evident in later Stoicism—even up to a certain point almost become a desire for death. It can be, at the same time, if not care for others, at least a care for one's self which will be beneficial to others. It is interesting to note in Seneca, for example, the importance of the theme: ''let us hasten to grow old, let us hasten to the appointed time which will permit us to rejoin our selves.'' This sort of moment before death, where nothing more can happen, is different from the desire for death that we find among Christians, who expect salvation from death. It is like a movement to articulate one's existence to the point where there would be nothing else before it but the possibility of death.

Q: We would now like to shift to another subject. In your courses at the Collège de France, you have talked about the relationships between power and knowledge. Now you talk about the relations between subject and truth. Is there a com- plementarity between the two sets of ideas: power/knowledge and subject/truth?

MF: My problem has always been, as I said in the beginning, the problem of the relationship between subject and truth. How does the subject enter into a certain game of truth? My first problem was, how is it, for example, that beginning at a certain point in time, madness was considered a problem and the result of a certain number of processes—an illness de- pendent upon a certain medicine? How has the mad subject been placed in this game of truth defined by knowledge or a medical model? And it is in doing this analysis that I noticed that, contrary to what had been somewhat the custom at that time—around the early sixties—it was not in talking simply about ideology that we could really explain that phenomenon. In fact, there were practices—essentially the major practice of confinement which had been developed at the beginning of the seventeenth century and which had been the condition for the insertion of the mad subject in this game of truth—which sent me back to the problem of institutions of power, much more than to the problem of ideology. So it was that I was led to pose the problem knowledge/power, which is not for me the fundamental problem but an instrument allowing the analysis—in a way that seems to me to be the most exact— of the problem of relationships between subject and games of truth.

Q: But you have always "refused" that we speak to you about the subject in general?

MF: No I had not "refused." I perhaps had some formulations which were inadequate. What I refused was precisely that you first of all set up a theory of the subject—as could be done in phenomenology and in existentialism—and that, beginning from the theory of the subject, you come to pose the question of knowing, for example, how such and such a form of knowledge was possible. What I wanted to know was how the subject constituted himself, in such and such a determined form, as a mad subject or as a normal subject, through a certain number of practices which were games of truth, applications of power, etc. I had to reject a certain *a priori* theory of the subject in order to make this analysis of the relationships which can exist between the constitution of the subject or different forms of the subject and games of truth, practices of power and so forth.

Q: That means that the subject is not a substance?

MF: It is not a substance; it is a form and this form is not above all or always identical to itself. You do not have towards yourself the same kind of relationships when you constitute yourself as a political subject who goes and votes or speaks up in a meeting, and when you try to fulfill your desires in a sexual relationship. There are no doubt some relationships and some interferences between these different kinds of subject but we are not in the presence of the same kind of subject. In each case, we play, we establish with one's self some different form of relationship. And it is precisely the historical constitution of these different forms of subject relating to games of truth that interest me.

10

michel foucault

Q: But the mad subject, the ill, the delinquent—perhaps even the sexual subject—was the subject which was the object of theoretical discourse, a subject shall we say "passive" while the subject of which you have been speaking for the last two years in your course at the Collège de France is an "active" subject, politically active. The care for self concerns all these problems of practical politics, of government, etc. It would seem that there has been a change in your thinking, a change not of perspective but of the problematic.

MF: If it is true, for example, that the constitution of a mad subject can in fact be considered as the result of a system of coercion—that is the passive subject—you know full well that the mad subject is not a non-free subject and that the mentally ill constitutes himself a mad subject in relationship and in the presence of the one who declares him crazy. Hysteria, which was so important in the history of psychiatry and in the mental institutions of the nineteenth century, seems to me to be the very illustration of the way in which the subject constitutes himself as mad. And it is not altogether a coincidence that the important phenomena of hysteria have been studied exactly where there was a maximum of coercion to compel these individuals to consider themselves mad. On the other hand and inversely, I would say that if now I am interested, in fact, in the way in which the subject constitutes himself in an active fashion, by the practices of self, these practices are nevertheless not something that the individual invents by himself. They are patterns that he finds in his culture and which are proposed, suggested and imposed on him by his culture, his society and his social group.

Q: There would seem to be a sort of lack in your problematic, namely, the concept of a resistance to power. That would presuppose a very active subject, very careful for self and of others and politically and philosophically sophisticated.

MF: That brings us back to the problem of what I mean by power. I hardly ever use the word "power" and if I do sometimes, it is always a short cut to the expression I always use: the relationships of power. But there are ready made patterns: when one speaks of "power," people think immediately of a political structure, a government, a dominant social class, the master facing the slave, and so on. That is not at all what I think when I speak of "relationships of power." I mean that in human relations, whatever they are—whether it be a question of communicating verbally, as we are doing right now, or a question of a love relationship, an institutional or economic relationship—power is always present: I mean the relationships in which one wishes to direct the behavior of another.

11

These are the relationships that one can find at different levels, under different forms: these relationships of power are changeable relations, i.e., they can modify themselves, they are not given once and for all. The fact, for example, that I am older and that at first you were intimidated can, in the course of the conversation, turn about and it is I who can become intimidated before someone, precisely because he is younger. These relations of power are then changeable, reversible and unstable. One must observe also that there cannot be relations of power unless the subjects are free. If one or the other were completely at the disposition of the other and became his thing, an object on which he can exercise an infinite and unlimited violence, there would not be relations of power. In order to exercise a relation of power, there must be on both sides at least a certain form of liberty. Even though the relation of power may be completely unbalanced or when one can truly say that he has "all power" over the other, a power can only be exercised over another to the extent that the latter still has the possibility of committing suicide, of jumping out of the window or of killing the other. That means that in the relations of power, there is necessarily the possibility of resistance, for if there were no possibility of resistance—of violent resistance, of escape, of ruse, of strategies that reverse the situation—there would be no relations of power. This being the general form, I refuse to answer the question that I am often asked: "But if power is everywhere, then there is no liberty."

I answer: if there are relations of power throughout every social field it is because there is freedom everywhere. Now there are effectively states of domination. In many cases the relations of power are fixed in such a way that they are perpetually asymetrical and the margin of liberty is extremely limited. To take an example, very paradigmatic to be sure: in the traditional conjugal relation in the society of the eighteenth and nineteenth centuries, we cannot say that there was only male power; the woman herself could do a lot of things: be unfaithful to him, extract money from him, refuse him sexually. She was, however, subject to a state of domination, in the measure where all that was finally no more than a certain number of tricks which never brought about a reversal of the situation. In these cases of domination—economic, social, institutional or sexual—the problem is in fact to find out where resistance is going to organize. Will this be, for example, a working class which is going to resist political domination—in the trade union, in the party—and under what form—a strike, a general strike, a revolution, a parliamentary struggle? In such a situation of domination, one must answer all these questions in a very specific fashion, in function of the kind and the precise form of domination. But the statement: "You see power everywhere, hence there is no place for liberty," seems to me to be absolutely incomplete. One cannot impute to me the idea that power is a system of domination which controls everything and which leaves no room for freedom.

Q: A short while ago you were talking about the free man and the philosopher, as if they were two different modalities of care for self. The philosopher's care for self would have a certain specificity and is not mistaken for that of the free man.

MF: I would say that it is a question of two different positions in the care for self, rather than two forms of the care for self. I think that care for self is the same in its form, but in intensity, in degree of zeal for self—and hence in zeal for others as well—the position of the philosopher is not that of any free man.

Q: Is that where one could expect a fundamental connection between philosophy and politics?

MF: Yes, of course. I think that the relationships between philosophy and politics are permanent and fundamental. It is certain that if one takes the history of the care for self in Greek thought, the relationships to politics is obvious. Under a very complex form: on the one hand, you see Socrates, for example—as well as Plato in the **Alcibiades**, as in Xenophon in the **Memorabilia**, who calls out to young people, "Hey, you, you want to become a political person, you want to govern the city, you therefore want to take care of others but you did not even take care of yourself, and if you do not take care for yourself, you will be a bad leader." In that perspective, the care for self appears like a pedagogical, moral and also ontological condition, for the constitution of a good leader. To constitute one's self as a subject who governs implies that one has constituted himself as a subject having care for self. But, on the other hand, you see Socrates who says in the **Apology**, "I, I hail everybody, because everybody must occupy himself with himself." But he immediately adds, "In doing this, I render the greatest service to the city and rather than punish me, you should reward me more than you reward a winner of the Olympic games." There is then a very strong affinity between philosophy and politics which will later develop itself, when the philosopher, in fact, will have not only the care of the soul of the citizen but also that of the prince.

Q: Could this problematic of the care for self become the center of a new philosophical thought, of another kind of politics than the one we are seeing today?

MF: I must admit that I have not gone very far in that direction and I would rather come back to some more contemporary problems, in order to try and see what we can do with all that in the actual political problematic. But I have the impression that in the political thought of the nineteenth century—and we might even have to go beyond, to Rousseau and Hobbes— the political subject has been thought essentially as subject to law, either in naturalist terms or in terms of positive law. In turn, it seems to me that the question of an ethical subject does not have much of a place in contemporary political thought. Finally, I don't like answering questions which I have not examined. I would, however, like to take up once again those questions which I have raised through the culture of Antiquity.

Q: What would be the relationship between the path of philosophy which leads to the knowledge of self and the path of spirituality?

MF: By spirituality, I understand—but I am not sure that it is a definition which we can hold for very long—that which precisely refers to a subject acceding to a certain mode of being and to the transformations which the subject must make of himself in order to accede to this mode of being. I believe that, in ancient spirituality, there was identity or almost so between spirituality and philosophy. In any case, the most important preoccupation of philosophy revolved about the self, the knowledge of the world coming afterwards, and, most of the time, as a support to this care for self. When you read Descartes, it is striking to find that in the **Méditations**, there is exactly this same spiritual care to accede to a mode of being where doubt would not be allowed and where finally we would know. But in thus defining the mode of being to which philosophy gives access, we notice that this mode of being is entirely determined by knowledge, and it is as access to a knowing subject or to what would qualify the subject as such that philosophy would define itself. And from that point of view, it seems to me that it superimposes the functions of spirituality on an ideal based on scientificity.

Q: Should we actualize this notion of care for self, in the classical sense, against this modern thought?

MF: Absolutely, but I am not doing that in order to say: "Unfortunately we have forgotten the care for self. Here is the care for self. It is the key to everything." Nothing is more foreign to me than the idea that philosophy strayed at a certain moment of time, and that it has forgotten something and that somewhere in her history there exists a principle, a basis that must be rediscovered. I think that all these forms of analysis, whether they take on a radical form by saying that from its point of departure, philosophy has been forgotten or whether it takes on a more historical form by saying, "See, in such michel foucault and such a philosopher something has been forgotten" are not very interesting. We cannot derive much from them. This does not mean that contact with such and such a philosopher cannot produce something but we would have to understand that this thing is new.

Q: That brings up the question. Why should we have access to truth today in the political sense, i.e., in the sense of political strategy confronting the various points of "blocking" or power in the relational system?

MF: That is in fact a problem. After all, why truth? And why are we concerned with truth, and more so than with the self? And why do we care for ourselves, only through the care for truth? I think that we are touching on a question which is very fundamental and which is, I would say, the question of the Western world. What caused all Western culture to begin to turn around this obligation of truth, which has taken on a variety of different forms? Things being what they are, nothing has, up to the present, proved that we could define a strategy exterior to it. It is indeed in this field of obligation to truth that we sometimes can avoid in one way or another the effects of a domination, linked to structures of truth or to institutions charged with truth. To say these things very schematically, we can find many examples: there has been an ecology move- ment—which is furthermore very ancient and is not only a twentieth century phenomenon—which has often been, in one sense, in hostile relationship with science or at least with a technology guaranteed in terms of truth. But in fact, ecology also spoke a language of truth. It was in the name of knowl- edge concerning nature, the equilibrium of the processes of living things, and so forth, that one could level the criticism. We escaped then a domination of truth, not by playing a game that was a complete stranger to the game of truth, but in playing it otherwise or in playing another game, another set, other trumps in the game of truth. I think it is the same thing in the order of politics, where we could criticize politics— beginning for example with the effects of the state of domi- nation of this undue politics—but we could only do this by playing a certain game of truth, showing what were the effects, showing that there were other rational possibilities, teaching people what they ignore about their own situation, on their conditions of work, on their exploitation.

Q: Concerning the question of the games of truth and the games of power, don't you think that one can find in history the presence of a particular modality of these games of truth which would have a particular status in respect to all other possibilities of games of truth and of power and which would be characterized by its essential openness, its opposition to all "blocking" of all power, to power in the sense of domination/bondage?

MF: Yes, absolutely. But, when I talk about relations of power and games of truth, I do not mean to say that the games of truth are but relationships of power that I would want to conceal—that would be a terrible caricature. My problem is, as I have already said, to know how games of truth can put themselves in place and be linked to relationships of power. We can show, for example, that the medicalization of madness, i.e., the organization of medical knowledge around individuals labeled as "mad," has been linked, at some time or other, to a whole series of social or economic processes, but also to institutions and practices of power. This fact in no way impairs the scientific validity of the therapeutic efficacy of psychiatry. It does not guarantee it but it does not cancel it out either. Let mathematics, for example, be linked—in an entirely different way than psychiatry—to structures of power; it would be equally true, even if it were only in the way it is taught, the manner in which the consensus of mathematicians organizes itself, functions in a closed circuit, has its values, determines what is good (true) and evil (false) in mathematics and so on. That does not at all mean that mathematics is only a game of power but that the game of truth of mathematics is linked, in a certain way and without impairing its validity, to games and to institutions of power. It is clear that in a certain number of cases the links are such that one can write the history of mathematics without bearing it in mind, even though this problematic is always interesting and now historians of mathematics are beginning to study the history of their institutions. Finally, it is clear that the relationship which can exist between the relations of power and the games of truth in mathematics is entirely different from the one you would have in psychiatry. In any case, one can in no way say that the games of truth are nothing else than games of power.

Q: This question goes back to the problem of the subject, for, in the games of truth, the question is asked: who says the truth, how is it said and why is it said? For, in the game of truth, you can play at saying the truth. There is one game—you play at truth or truth is a game.

MF: The word "game" can lead you into error: when I say "game" I mean an ensemble of rules for the production of the truth. It is not a game in the sense of imitating or entertaining ... it is an ensemble of procedures which lead to a certain result, which can be considered in function of its principles and its rules of procedures, as valid or not, as winner or loser.

michel foucault

Q: There is always the problem of the who. Is it a group, an ensemble?

MF: It can be a group, an individual. There is indeed a problem there. You can observe, insofar as the multiple games of truth are concerned, that what has always characterized our society, since the time of the Greeks, is the fact that we do not have a complete and peremptory definition of the games of truth which would be allowed, to the exclusion of all others. There is always a possibility, in a given game of truth, to discover something else and to more or less change such and such a rule and sometimes even the totality of the game of truth. No doubt that is what has given the West, in relationship to other societies, possibilities of development that we find nowhere else. Who says the truth? Individuals who are free, who arrive at a certain agreement and who find themselves thrust into a certain network of practices of power and constraining institutions.

Q: Truth then is not a construct?

MF: That depends. There are some games of truth in which truth is a construct and others when it is not. You can have, for example, a game of truth which consists in describing things in such a way. The one who gives an anthropological description of society does not give us a construct, but a description—which has, as far as it is concerned—a certain number of rules, evolving historically, so that one can say that up to a certain point it is a construct in relationship to another description. That does not mean that there is nothing there and that everything comes out of somebody's head. Of what we can say, for example, of this transformation of games of truth, some draw the conclusion that I said that nothing existed—I have been made to say that madness does not exist, although the problem was quite the contrary. It was a question of knowing how madness, under the various definitions that we could give it, could be at a certain moment, integrated in an institutional field which considered it a mental illness, occupying a certain place alongside other illnesses.

Q: Basically there is also a problem of communication at the heart of the problem of truth, the problem of the transparence of the words of speech. The one who can formulate truths also has a power, the power of being able to say the truth and to express it as he wishes.

MF: Yes, and that does not mean however that what he says is not true, as most people believe. When you point out to them that there can be a relation between truth and power, they say: "Ah good! then it is not the truth."

17

Q: That goes along with the problem of communication, for in a society where communication has a high level of transparence, the games of truth are perhaps more independent of the structures of power.

MF: You are posing a very important problem there: I think you are referring to Habermas as you say that. I am interested in what Habermas is doing. I know that he does not agree with what I say—I am a little more in agreement with him—but there is always something which causes me a problem. It is when he assigns a very important place to relations of communication and also a function that I would call "utopian." The thought that there could be a state of communication which would be such that the games of truth could circulate freely, without obstacles, without constraint and without coercive effects, seems to me to be Utopia. It is being blind to the fact that relations of power are not something bad in themselves, from which one must free one's self. I don't believe there can be a society without relations of power, if you understand them as means by which individuals try to conduct, to determine the behavior of others. The problem is not of trying to dissolve them in the utopia of a perfectly transparent communication, but to give one's self the rules of law, the techniques of management, and also the ethics, the *ethos*, the practice of self, which would allow these games of power to be played with a minimum of domination.

Q: You are far removed from Sartre who used to tell us "Power is evil."

MF: Yes, and that idea has often been attributed to me, which is very far from what I think. Power is not an evil. Power is strategic games. We know very well indeed that power is not an evil. Take for example, sexual relationship or love relationships. To exercise power over another, in a sort of open strategic game, where things could be reversed, that is not evil. That is part of love, passion, of sexual pleasure. Let us also take something that has been the object of criticism, often justified: the pedagogical institution. I don't see where evil is in the practice of someone who, in a given game of truth, knowing more than another, tells him what he must do, teaches him, transmits knowledge to him, communicates skills to him. The problem is rather to know how you are to avoid in these practices—where power cannot not play and where it is not evil in itself—the effects of domination which will make a child subject to the arbitrary and useless authority of a teacher, or put a student under the power of an abusively authoritarian professor, and so forth. I think these problems should be posed in terms of rules of law, of relational tech-

michel foucault niques of government and of *ethos*, of practice of self and of freedom.

Q: Can we understand what you have just said to be the fundamental criteria of what you have called a new ethics? It would be a question of playing with the minimum of domination. . . .

MF: I think that in fact there is the point of articulation of the ethical preoccupation and of the political struggle for the respect of rights, of the critical reflexion against the abusive techniques of government and of the ethical research which allows individual liberty to be founded.

Q: When Sartre speaks of power as supreme evil, he seems to refer to the reality of power as domination. You probably agree with Sartre on that?

MF: I think that all those notions have been ill-defined and we don't really know what we are talking about. Myself, I am not sure, when I began to interest myself in this problem of power, of having spoken very clearly about it or used the words needed. Now I have a much clearer idea of all that. It seems to me that we must distinguish the relationships of power as strategic games between liberties—strategic games that result in the fact that some people try to determine the conduct of others— and the states of domination, which are what we ordinarily call power. And, between the two, between the games of power and the states of domination, you have governmental technologies—giving this term a very wide meaning for it is also the way in which you govern your wife, your children, as well as the way you govern an institution. The analysis of these techniques is necessary, because it is often through this kind of technique that states of domination are established and maintain themselves. In my analysis of power, there are three levels: the strategic relationships, the techniques of government, and the levels of domination.

Q: We find in your course on the Hermeneutic of the Subject a passage where you say that there is no other principal and useful point of resistance to political power than in the relationship of self to self.

MF: I do not think that the only point of possible resistance to political power—understand of course, as a state of domination—lies in the relationship of self to self. I say that governmentality implies the relationship of self to self, which means exactly that, in the idea of governmentality, I am aiming at the totality of practices, by which one can constitute, define, organize, instrumentalize the strategies which individuals in their liberty can have in regard to each other. It is free individuals

19

who try to control, to determine, to delimit the liberty of others and, in order to do that, they dispose of certain instruments to govern others. That rests indeed on freedom, on the relationship of self to self and the relationship to the other. But if you try to analyze power not from the point of view of liberty, of strategies and of governmentality but from the point of view of a political institution, you cannot consider the subject as a subject of rights. We have a subject who was endowed with rights or who was not and who, by the institution of a political society, has received or has lost rights. You are then thrown back to a juridical concept of the subject. On the other hand, the notion of governmentality allows one, I believe, to set off the freedom of the subject and the relationship to others, i.e., that which constitutes the very matter of ethics.

Q: Do you think philosophy has anything to say on the **why** of this tendency to want to determine the conduct of others?

MF: This manner of determining the conduct of others will take very different forms, will arouse appetites and desires of varying intensity according to societies. I don't know anything about anthropology but we can imagine that there are societies in which the way one determines the behaviour of others is so well determined in advance, that there is nothing left to do. On the other hand, in a society like ours—it is very evident in family relationships, for example, in sexual and affective relations— the games can be extremely numerous and thus the temptation to determine the conduct of others is that much greater. However, the more that people are free in respect to each other, the greater the temptation on both sides to determine the conduct of others. The more open the game, the more attractive and fascinating it is.

Q: Do you think philosophy has the duty of sounding a warning on the danger of power?

MF: That duty has always been an important function of philosophy. On the critical side—I mean critical in a very broad sense—philosophy is precisely the challenging of all phenomena of domination at whatever level or under whatever form they present themselves—political, economic, sexual, institutional, and so on. This critical function of philosophy, up to a certain point, emerges right from the socratic imperative: "Be concerned with yourself, i.e., ground yourself in liberty, through the mastery of self."

Boston College

karlis racevskis

michel foucault, rameau's nephew, and the question of identity

Of all the paradoxes entertained and cultivated by Michel Foucault in his writings, none is probably more intractable—and pervasive—than the notion of identity. This question of identity is, after all, the one that arises inevitably when we consider the relation between the work and the author—a relation that is also, as Foucault himself has shown, a function of history and language.

The paradox is the following: identity is what is naturally given and is therefore considered as a possession, yet it is also that which possesses the individual. If, on the one hand, identity is constituted by a personal experience and an individual history, it is also and inevitably a product of the otherness of cultural, social, and linguistic determinants. As the individual reconstructs and reflects upon an imaginary identity, he/she cultivates an illusion of conscious control that only serves to occlude the aleatory and contingent nature of this imaginary essence. Thus, in a sense, identity is our metaphysical refuge, it is the gap between our history and History, between our self-conscious and purposeful use of language and the *Logos* that makes our speech possible. We reside in this gap by covering it up with an explanatory system that reconciles our self-image with our being, a system that has also the virtue of placing other humans within the context of a fundamental nature, a teleological design, or a scientific paradigm.

Foucault's project can be viewed as an attempt to dramatize and to magnify this gap. To do this, he operates a fundamental reversal and, instead of starting with what is traditionally considered as the given, applies his archaeological and genealogical analyses to whatever is deemed normal and natural. The purpose is not only to effectuate a separation between thought and essence, between language and being, but also to demonstrate the inevitable and intricate coexistence of the two seemingly mutually exclusive realms. We are thus made to understand that thought contains that which contains **it** as well; it is shaped by that to which it can only tentatively, gropingly attempt to give shape in turn. Thought and thought-of-self thus partake of the same paradox and the delusions of self-sufficient thought are those of an identity that claims a sovereign and purposeful role in an individual's destiny.

Foucault's critique of identity is therefore not to be taken as a simple manifestation of his own identity, that is, as an outgrowth of a very personal desire for anonymity, expressed in the well-known admonition "do not ask who I am and do not ask me to remain the same."[1] To do so would be to attribute to Foucault's argument a circularity that would, in effect, invalidate the critical force of his discourse.[2] Rather, this critique should be seen as a basic component of Foucault's intellectual strategy: we write, he says, "to be other than what we are."[3] Thus, the intellectual curiosity that has motivated his archaeological and genealogical pursuits is "not the kind that seeks to assimilate whatever is appropriate to know, but the kind that allows one to take oneself away from oneself [*se déprendre de soi-même*]." The purpose of writing has therefore been to "know to what extent the exercise of thinking one's own history can free thought from what it thinks silently and to allow it to think otherwise."[4]

The motif of "*penser autrement*" is a familiar one in Foucault's work and is to be found there from the earliest publications. It is most explicit when Foucault speaks of himself and his writing. His characterization of his own subjectivity expresses a duality that derives from the realization that "to speak is to do something—something other than to express what one thinks, to translate what one knows."[5] On the other hand, Foucault also acknowledges the massive indoctrination to which, he realizes, he has been subjected. The metaphorical expressiveness of such statements as "I have been bottle-fed with knowledge," and "I have muddled about in knowledge"[6] suggest the keenness of Foucault's self-consciousness with regard to the educational and cultural nurturing he underwent. This awareness brings with it the inescapable corollary, which is a rejection of an identity derived from this culture and education. The rejection is all the more pronounced because such an identity is closely bound to the notion of essence, of being, and is consequently to be considered a product of the epistemological configuration that gave rise to the figure of "man" at the beginning of the nineteenth century. Identity is therefore inextricably enmeshed in

22

political strategies and involved with the power/knowledge effects applied by discourse.

One of the minor controversies with which Foucault-scholarship has occasionally been concerned is the question of the nature of Foucault's project: is Foucault the theoretician of the subject or of power? Foucault himself has at times felt obliged to clarify his stance, although the positions he has taken on this question have varied. The whole question is probably moot because, to put it simply, Foucault **has** to be concerned with both power and the subject since the theoretical importance of any one of the two elements is directly related to the existence of the other. What Foucault's analyses propose is an understanding of the process through which subjects are formed. Thus, a subject is that which is amenable to the effects of power: it is the handle by which power takes a hold of/on individual human beings. For power to be effective, humans have to be subjected in the name of their being—that is, there has to be a "being" serving as an alibi if the process of subjection is to be effective. Being, in turn, is but an effect of discourse that naturalizes the situation of individuals in the universe, in history, or in a collective destiny.

In the prefatory remarks to **L'usage des plaisirs**, Foucault explains that his purpose is to study the manner in which humans are constituted historically in terms of an experience that not only **can** but also **must** be perceived as such; to do this, he has undertaken an analysis of "the games of truth," of "the interplay of truth and falsehood through which being is constituted historically as experience, that is, as something that can and must be thought."[7] This means that the cognitive threshold that allows us to conceptualize something as an experience is also the one marking our entry into the field of ethical valorization. This means also that this notion of experience that everyone takes for granted turns out to be a rather complicated phenomenon. Thus, for example, Foucault sees the experience of sexuality as constituted along the three different axes that make up an appropriate domain of *savoir*: the discursive practices that articulate this field of knowledge; the strategies of normalization and techniques of rationalization that allow for the application of power; the forms that pattern an individual's relation to himself or herself allowing the individual to recognize himself or herself as a subject—in other words, the process that gives rise to an identity.

Now the process through which subjects and their identities are constituted is one that is deeply ingrained in culture, one that is immanent in the dominant epistemological mode of the modern period in particular. It is also a basically duplicitous process because it is predicated on a necessary delusion: the evidence necessary for interpreting experience is produced by a precritical stage of experience: "The precritical analysis of what man is in his essence becomes the analytic of everything that can, in general be presented to man's experience."[8] It is this essence or being of man that furnishes the necessary authority for legitimizing a discourse on experience. In order to change this pattern, it is necessary to remove the fundamental element on which its functioning depends, it is necessary to invalidate this alibi of an essence and to imagine "what the world and thought and truth might be if man did not exist."[9]

To escape the delusion nurtured by the modern *epistémé,* it is essential that the "anthropological prejudice" be uncovered and discredited and a general critique of reason be undertaken. The figures of Hölderlin, Nerval, Nietzsche, Roussel, and Artaud are exemplary in this sense. Foucault has also singled out the critical importance of Diderot's short masterpiece **Le Neveu de Rameau** in this context, finding that the insights offered by the fictional creation of the *philosophe* have a prophetic importance:

The laughter of Rameau's Nephew prefigures and reduces in advance the whole anthropological movement of the nineteenth century; in all of post-Hegelian thought, man will proceed from certitude to truth through the efforts of mind and reason; but long before already, Diderot had let it be understood that man is ceaselessly thrown back from reason to the untrue truth of the immediate, and this by means of an effortless mediation, a mediation always already operative since the beginning of time. This impatient mediation, which is both extreme distance and absolute promiscuity, entirely negative because it has only a subversive force, but completely positive, because it is fascinated in that which it suppresses, this mediation is the delirium of unreason—the enigmatic figure in which we recognize madness.[10]

The persona of the young Rameau constitutes an effective critical device because it is an individual unlike all others around him. Rameau is not part of the system, his perspective places him clearly outside the realm of culture and its norms—yet without severing his ties completely, since he still depends on it for survival. What separates Rameau from others is, as Foucault observes, his complete inability to be a hypocrite. Likewise, Diderot tells us that, "neither more nor less detestable than other men, he was franker than they, more logical, and thus often profound in his depravity."[11] Rameau has vices but escapes moral condemnation because of the guilelessness with which he cultivates these. He is a mask without a soul: "I have never in my life thought before speaking, nor while speaking, nor after speaking. The upshot is, I offend nobody" (**RN**, p.47). It is this depth of Rameau's depravity that Foucault finds revealing because it stands in stark contrast with the imaginary depths of humanistic rationales.

In the first place, Rameau's rantings have the effect of disclosing the pretentiousness of Reason and its claims to Truth. As Rameau observes, whatever knowledge we possess is but an infinitesimal part of the vast symbolic realm of possibility; consequently, to be able to claim to know anything well, we would have to know everthing, because "until one knows everything, one knows nothing worth knowing; ignorant of the origin of this, the purpose of that, and the place of either. Which should come first? Can one teach without method? And where does method spring from? I tell you, Philosopher mine, I have an idea physics will always be a puny science, a drop of water picked up from the great ocean on the point of a needle, a grain of dust from the Alps" (**RN**, p.29).

Once ascertained and disclosed, the limitations of our knowledge and its pretense of systematic arrangement bring with it inescapable consequences for the existing system of morality: they produce the realization that distinctions between true and false have their inevitable counterpart in distinctions between good and evil, between virtue and vice. Truth, as Foucault has shown, is ultimately political in nature and is predicated on knowledge/power strategies operative in a given society and age. Truth in this regard has not set humans free but has instituted subjection, since "the man described for us, whom we are invited to free, is already in himself the effect of a subjection much more profound than himself. A 'soul' inhabits him and brings him to existence, which is itself a factor in the mastery that power exercises over the body. The soul is the effect and instrument of a political anatomy; the soul is the prison of the body."[12] Subjection, in a moral as well as in a physical sense, is carried out by means of a dual functioning of discourse which, on the one hand, socializes bodies by making them amenable to the effects of a second purpose— which is the definition and organization of the restraints and coercions to be applied. There are, of course, the ever-present areas of self-interest that are coopted by the process in the name of certain truths. This is accomplished through an appeal to a reason capable of discerning truths by virtue of its disinterested and "objective" nature. But, as Rameau well knows, superior truths, morality, and the officially recognized values are no more than useful pretenses and constitute masks to be worn when the occasion demands. The fact is that "virtue is praised, but hated. People run away from it, for it is ice-cold and in this world you must keep your feet warm" (**RN**, p.38). Virtue, justice, the laws establishing virtue and justice are purely decorative: there are other, more effective laws that determine the unfolding of events; to deal effectively with reality, it is these laws that one must respect. Thus it is essential to remember that "in a subject as variable as manners and morals, nothing is absolutely, essentially, universally true or false—unless it be that one must be whatever self-interest requires, good or bad, wise or foolish, decent or ridiculous, honest or vicious" (**RN**, p.50). It is this awareness that will put us in tune with the general law of nature to which human existence is subject, to the fundamental principle according to which "in Nature all species live off one another; in society all classes do the same. We square things up with one another without benefit of the law" (**RN**, p.33). It all comes down to a matter of survival then and one needs to live in a manner that accomodates both levels of social reality—the power/knowledge mechanisms as well as the official axiological and cultural scheme.

Thus Rameau notes that "each profession makes exceptions to universal morality," exceptions that he calls "trade idioms" (**RN**, p.32). Vice is not inherently harmful—only its appearances are. Rameau has therefore made a systematic study of various vices that can be useful provided they remain concealed from public view. And yet, in spite of Rameau's insights and superior understanding, in spite of his application in the study of useful behavior, he is, curiously, a *raté*; Diderot presents him as someone destined to fail in all his attempts to become rich and famous. Rameau's strategy is doomed to remain ineffective because he is incapable of cultivating the one quality that would allow him to successfully reconcile a superficial morality with the fundamental laws of self-interest: he is incapable of hypocrisy. *Moi* tells him, "you'll never be happy if the pros and cons weigh with you equally. You should make up your mind and stick to it" (**RN**, p.13). Rameau is too lucid to "make up his mind" and it is this lucidity that makes him one of the most appealing creations of the eighteenth century. His humanity has a directness and profoundness that manifests itself in observations that capture some of the more radical aspects of Enlightenment thought: "I find that it is no part of good order to be sometimes without food. What a hell of an economy! Some men replete with everything while others, whose stomachs are no less importunate, whose hunger is just as recurrent, have nothing to bite on" (**RN**, p.82).

26 Such a perspective on human affairs implicitly rejects the foreclosures imposed by existing rationales. Rameau's genius, or rather that of Diderot, is thus remarkable for the insistence with which it maintains an opening toward the otherness of unreason, toward the possibility of a dimension that Reason will attempt to ignore or colonize as "madness" in the following century. As Foucault observes:

When we consider . . . that the project of Descartes was to tolerate doubt provisionally until truth appeared in the reality of evident ideas, we can see that the non-Cartesian component of modern thought, in its most decisive aspect, does not begin with a discussion of innate ideas, or the incrimination of the ontological argument, but indeed with this text of Rameau's Nephew, with this existence it designates in a reversal that was not to be understood before the time of Hölderlin and Hegel.[13]

In the light of Foucault's analysis, Diderot's work not only reveals the pattern of thought that was going to make it possible for humans to become the objects of positive knowledge but also analyzes the authorial function in a manner that avoids the lure of facile correspondences with the identity of a literary figure called Diderot. Instead of discovering the presence of a biographical subject, we find ourselves in a position to discern a creative consciousness that has assimilated and reproduced the characteristic configuration of an archive, producing a discourse that maintains itself in the precarious and imprecise area separating the Same from the Other. By analyzing **Rameau's Nephew** as something that mediates between the Other and the authorial self, Foucault's text reveals a dimension that consistently undermines the claims of any systematic or "objective" reconstruction of the human experience, an experience shaped by a cognitive dimension—a *savoir*—that gives shape to our thought in imperceptible ways.

Foucault's attitude toward this *savoir* is ambiguous. It is a realm at the limits of consciousness that can both fascinate with its power to mold and incite as well as alienate with its potential for control and oppression. The justification for this ambivalence is to be found in the realization that all knowledge derives from a dimension both profound and elusive with which it is organically linked: "In a society, all knowledge, philosophical ideas, everyday opinions, but also institutions, commercial and police practices, customs, everything is related to a certain *savoir* that is implicit in and characteristic of this society."[14]

This *savoir* is thus a condition of possibility, a cognitive matrix that organizes different fields of knowledge and legitimates truths. When truths cease to command a general adherence, the underlying epistemological organization of an epoch becomes vulnerable to critique: the obsolescent condition of the disintegrating "order of things" is all the more criticable when it continues to hold a partial sway over the critic. It is in this conjunction that a critique of culture becomes, at the same time, an attempt to escape identity, to get away from oneself— an injunction to "*se déprendre de soi.*"

Foucault does not deny that the desire to "*se déprendre de soi*" is an imperative that has its roots in some very personal experiences. It has something to do, for example, with a growing feeling of alienation toward some intellectual currents whose stifling domination Foucault experienced in his youth; he explains: "I belong to a generation of people who, when they were students, were shut in within the boundaries of a horizon demarcated by Marxism, phenomenology, existentialism, etc. All very interesting, stimulating things but which, after a while, bring on a feeling of suffocation and the desire to go look somewhere else."[15] In a similar manner, recalling his early professional involvement with psychiatry, Foucault remembers vividly the sensation of being an outsider, of not being able to think according to and within the accepted codes of psychiatric knowledge. He remembers, for example, the suffering he experienced at the sight of the inmates' suffering, a feeling of empathy that contrasted sharply with the scientific impassivity of the doctors.[16] What he calls his "good fortune" of finding himself in a psychiatric hospital "neither as a patient nor as a doctor" gave him also the opportunity to observe the goings on with "a somewhat empty, a somewhat neutral gaze . . . outside the codes . . . to become conscious of this extremely strange reality of confinement."[17] The distance provided by his disinvolvement gave him a vantage from which he was able to observe the professionals in action. What struck Foucault was the manner in which the act of confining human beings was taken as something perfectly natural, as a procedure whose legitimacy was self-evident. The naturalness of this power to subject others led him to reflect on the long historical process that had yielded the necessary truths for institutionalizing procedures of confinement. In a sense then, the alienation, even revulsion occasioned by certain ways of applying knowledge made Foucault eager to examine more closely the history, mechanisms, and effects of this knowledge.

It is of course relatively recently that Foucault arrived at such a comprehensive understanding of the motives that guided the writing of his earlier works in particular. At the same time, it is significant that it is also in the light of these earlier experiences that he explains the most recent project on sexuality noting that too much has been made of a supposed contrast between his earlier and his later writings. "I have said nothing different from what I was already saying," he observes and points out that by studying the manner of "governing" the insane, he was attempting to connect the "constitution of the experience of the self by someone insane, within the framework of mental illness, to psychiatric practice and the institution of the asylum." In his books on sexuality, he wanted to "show how the governing of the self is integrated in a practice of governing others." In both cases, the aim was the same because it was to find out "how an 'experience' made up of the relations to self and others is constituted."[18]

What is noteworthy here is that the problematic of the subject has been extended to include a consideration of "others." The question of the subject had always been a central one in Foucault's work but it became especially crucial when he discovered that the problematization of the subject becomes an issue only with the advent of Christianity. The constitution of the self as subject had evidently not been considered a problem in antiquity because, although there was a *mode d'assujettissement*—a mode of subjection, it was something that did not operate so much according to moral norms as it depended on an aesthetic choice or a political system. What intrigued Foucault at this juncture was the process of transformation that led from a highly personalized ethic to the Christian kind of morality with its interdictions and normalizing effects.

Foucault was indeed looking for a connection and considering the two eras in question—antiquity and early Christianity—not so much in terms of a break separating them but from the perspective of a continuity to be found in a transposition of elements. These elements, although different when considered separately, fit into patterns that performed the same function for both ages. Thus, although the notion of discontinuity had always been an important methodological tool for Foucault, he points out that its significance has been exaggerated by critics and singles out the notion of problematization as the thematic thread linking all his analyses to a common purpose. The point is not to find divergences and to bring out oppositions but to gain a better understanding of cultural processes by trying to see, as much as possible, the whole panorama—both synchronically and diachronically—because, "it is the ensemble of discursive and non-discursive practices which brings something to the interplay of truths and falsehoods constituting it into an object of thought."[19] It is then the comparative approach that is the most likely to furnish a different grasp of the *savoir* that oversees knowledge/power formations and determines a cultural identity. It is also in this context that

the knowledges that Foucault resurrects become useful: they

are neither exemplary nor privileged but serve to alter acquired and naturalized perspectives. Thus, when Foucault talks of the Greeks it is not to present them as models for a lifestyle. Indeed, considering the elitism, the institution of slavery, the exclusiveness of male privilege that characterize Greek society, Foucault admits to a feeling of contempt for the Greek ethics of pleasure, which he sees irrevocably "linked to a virile society, to nonsymmetry, exclusion of the Other, an obsession with penetration, and a kind of threat of being dispossessed of your own energy, and so on."[20] However, when the Greek episode becomes an integral component of the genealogy of a specific problematic, it has a valuable contribution to make to a current perception of subjectivity. For example, Foucault discovers that "the great changes which occurred between Greek society, Greek ethics, Greek morality and how the Christians viewed themselves are not in the code but are in what I call the 'ethics,' the relation to oneself."[21] This relation to oneself has been the unstated, unacknowledged part of a massive *savoir* whose visible manifestation is the code that stipulates what is forbidden and what is not. To see a pattern in the way transformations have taken place not in the code but in the manner a relation to oneself is conceived can be helpful in understanding the nature of present-day approaches to the problem of ethics. Foucault thinks that in this sense our problem could be similar to that of the Greeks "since most of us no longer believe that ethics is founded in religion"; our concerns are more like those of the ancient Greeks because "in Greek ethics people were concerned with their moral conduct, their ethics, their relations to themselves and to others much more than with religious problems."[22] Thus Foucault brings out once more the impossibility of considering separately a relation to oneself and that to others and concludes that the Christian model, understood as "a moral experience centered on the subject no longer seems satisfactory."[23]

In the case of Foucault's own relation to himself, of his self-perception as intellectual in particular, the problematization is similar. The effort to "make oneself permanently able to remove oneself from oneself" [*se rendre capable en permanence de se déprendre de soi-même*] has, as its corollary, a concomitant effort to involve others. Consequently, "this effort to modify your own thinking and that of others . . . seems to be the intellectual's *raison d'être*."[24] The intellectual's purpose is not to propose models or to

shape the political will of others; it is . . . to reexamine evidences and postulates, to shake up habits, ways of doing and thinking, to dissipate accepted familiarities, to reexamine rules and institutions, and by taking as a starting point this reprob-

30

lematization (in which he plays his specific role of intellectual) to take part in the formation of a political will (where he has his role of citizen to play).[25]

This reaffirmation of the already familiar choice of specific over the universal intellectual stance brings up the theme of identity once more— but with an additional specification: that of citizenship. According to Foucault, the intellectual is someone involved with concrete issues and subject to the same constraints as other citizens. The awareness of these constraints joined to the desire to elucidate them give the intellectual's task its specificity. This task, which is at once an effort to lift subjection by displaying its mechanisms and to remove oneself from oneself by undertaking to constantly transform one's own thinking is also an attempt to locate the intellectual's freedom at the point of his/her limitations—the point at which desire meets with processes of subjectivization, the place where identity forms. To elucidate these processes, the appropriate questions to ask are the following: "Who makes decisions for me? Who keeps me from doing one thing and tells me to do something else? Who programs my movements and my schedule? Who forces me to live at this particular place while I work at this other one? How are these decisions that completely articulate my life made?"[26] There are two observations to be made with regard to Foucault's choice of questions. First, they are not asked in order to uncover a specific identity, a person, group, or class lurking behind each "who"; an attempt or claim to do this would be that of a "universal" intellectual. For Foucault, there are no strategists to be identified behind the strategies—no one occupies the place of the Other. Nevertheless, it is in the name of the Other that identities are formed; by questioning the provenance of the forces that control an individual's life, Foucault calls into question the accepted patterns of individualization.

Secondly, the questions suggested by Foucault are the kind that anyone could ask and yet they are a highly improbable sort of questions: they go counter to some of the most deeply ingrained and culturally conditioned assumptions concerning individual freedom and responsibility. Thus it is the intellectual's obligation to make others aware of questions and possibilities that some would call unacceptable or inconceivable. The problematization of the intellectual's role is inextricably linked to the problematization of the place humans occupy in society, a place designated and defined by a cultural and social order; the "*souci de soi*" is but an integral part of a "*souci des autres.*" Foucault once characterized his intellectual stance as one of "hyper- and pessimistic activism."[27] It is a description that alludes to the unresolvable tension between sameness and alterity, between identity and the desire to be different that characterize the place of the intellectual's questioning in Foucault's work. There are no solutions or victories to be anticipated, only a constant resistance to be maintained—one we find expressed once more on the back cover of Foucault's last two books, in a quotation from the poet René Char: "*L'histoire des hommes est la longue succession des synonymes d'un même vocable. Y contredire est un devoir.*"

Wright State University

NOTES

1. Michel Foucault, **The Archaeology of Knowledge**, tr. A.M. Sheridan Smith (New York: Pantheon Books, 1972), p.17.

2. Some of the criticism directed at Foucault over the years has taken the form of precisely this sort of argument and has attempted to reconsider Foucault's contribution as a reflection of certain misguided and deplorable tendencies in contemporary culture. The reader is of course required to assume that the authors of such critiques have the necessary vision to be the spokespersons for the sane and healthy tendencies of the age.

3. "Archéologie d'une passion," **Magazine littéraire** 221 (July-August 1985), p.104. Interview with Michel Foucault conducted by Charles Ruas.

4. Michel Foucault, **L'usage des plaisirs** (Paris: Gallimard, 1984), pp. 14 & 15. My translation.

5. **The Archaeology of Knowledge**, p. 209

6. **Radioscopie de Jacques Chancel**, Cassettes Radio France (3 March, 1975). Interview with Michel Foucault.

7. **L'usage des plaisirs**, pp. 12–13. My translation of the following: "*des jeux du vrai et du faux à travers lesquels l'être se constitue historiquement comme expérience, c'est-à-dire comme pouvant et devant être pensé.*"

8. Michel Foucault, **The Order of Things** (New York: Vintage Books, 1973), p. 341.

9. **Ibid**. p. 322

10. Michel Foucault, **Histoire de la folie à l'âge classique** (Paris: Gallimard, 1972), pp. 370–71. My translation.

11. Denis Diderot, **Rameau's Nephew and Other Works**, tr. Jacques Barzun and Ralph H. Bowen (New York: Bobbs-Merrill, 1964), p. 74. Henceforth this work will be identified parenthetically within the text as **RN**.

12. Michel Foucault, **Discipline and Punish**, tr. Alan Sheridan (New York: Pantheon, 1978), p. 30.

13. **Histoire de la folie**, p. 368. My translation.

14. Raymond Bellour, **Le livre des autres** (Paris: U.G.E, 1978), p. 15. Interview with Michel Foucault conducted in 1967. My translation.

32 15. "Archéologie d'une passion," p. 105. My translation.

16. **Radioscopie de Jacques Chancel.**

17. "Du pouvoir," **L'Express** (13 July, 1984), p. 56. Interview by Pierre Boncenne. My translation.

18. "Le souci de la vérité", **Magazine littéraire** 207 (May 1984), pp. 18 & 21. Interview by Francois Ewald. My translation.

19. **Ibid**. p. 18.

20. "How We Behave," **Vanity Fair** (November 1983), p. 63. Interview by Paul Rabinow and Hubert L. Dreyfus.

21. **Ibid**. p. 66.

22. **Ibid**. p. 62.

23. "Final Interview," **Raritan** 5:1 (Summer 1985), p. 12. Interview by Gilles Barbette.

24. "Le souci de la vérité", p. 22.

25. **Ibid**.

26. "Du pouvoir", p. 60.

27. "How We Behave", p. 62.

garth gillan

foucault's philosophy

The writings of Michel Foucault present a singular challenge to retrospective interpretation, for their interpretation cannot bypass the conditions that Foucault himself laid down. Neither author, nor *oeuvre*; neither intentionality, nor constitutive subjectivity; neither experience, nor linear history, can, according to Foucault's critique of intellectual history and the phenomenological theory of language, provide the categories around which interpretation can be formulated. Can one even, then, speak of Foucault? Is there an author and an *oeuvre*? Is there a fundamental intention or project animating the course of Foucault's works? Do they compose a specific history with its external limits and internal contours? And if those questions must be answered in the negative, is it sufficient to respond that one must present a Foucauldian interpretation of Foucault, as it was once proposed that only a Marxist interpretation can be given of Marx?

The incisiveness of those questions is reflected in the fact that Foucault's works are seen to lie, on the one hand, in a hermeneutic structuralism, or, on the other, in specific analyses without any intention to formulate a general theory of categories those analyses utilize.[1]

Where do Foucault's own progressive/retrogressive reflections, to borrow from J.P. Sartre, lie along the above axes? Clearly Foucault took this matter very seriously, for the course of his works is marked by methodological shifts, modifications, and self-critique, agonizingly articulated, frankly defended and brutally stated with great force. Foucault's writings institutionalize a certain violence that belongs to the texts themselves and is part of their self-consciousness. Discontinuity in the concept of method is one of the marks of that violence. Not by addition or the gradual accumulation of new data and perspectives do Foucault's works move beyond their predecessors, but by calling into question their legitimacy. Foucault is a question for Foucault.

Foucault has no Parsonian general theory of society, nor a universal theory of history. But, on the other hand, he poses a set of questions that interpenetrate, transform and fructify one another; that succeed one another in the course of time without abolishing their succession; and finally establish a discourse among themselves. A discourse among questions. This is more than an interrogative discourse that models itself after exploration in the perceptual world. It has a different model: politics, the effects of questions on the destabilization of power networks. Foucault's works involve the discursive practice of the question: a practice that arises from the space of social practice embedded in institutions, disciplines and sexual behavior.

Logic is not the model for theory for Foucault; discourse is. Logical theory assumes a hierarchy of concepts in relationships of subordination and dependence, whose implications follow from universal concepts. Discourse involves a heterogeneity in its practice: it traverses a space with irreducible origins, non-universalizable locales, and is marked by a history in which events overturn other events and institutions arise on the basis of the violence done to that which sustains them in the materiality, principally, the body. Discourse is the domain of the irreducibility of the distance between question and answer: the distance that creates dialectic. What is striking in Foucault's writings is the presence of a desire that, similar to Plato's, animates or underscores the dialectic of question and answer, but, in contrast to that of Plato's, does not gravitate around the axes of poverty and plenty, the absence or presence of absolute being. Foucault's desire is a nomadic desire, desire that signifies in the moment of transgression, *eros.* Foucault's discourse signifies at the point where limits are crossed, discontinuity irrupts in the midst of continuity, and violence twists signs into unforeseen shapes. A nomadic desire that takes discourse for its object, and through discourse reaches the unrecognizable: a genealogy of the body that touches the nerve of its desire as it has been inscribed, by means of words or instruments of torture, in disciplines, institutions, discursive practices, and sexuality. In **The Use of Pleasure**,[2] this nomadic desire surfaces as a curiosity that rejects the dominance that any object proper to itself would have over knowledge, and lays emphasis upon "that which enables one to get free of oneself."[3] This "curiosity" explains the reason why the two latest volumes in **The History of Sexuality** have modified the program of the original volume. In a mood of self-reflection, Foucault writes: "There are times in life when the question of knowing if one can think differently than one thinks, and perceive differently than one sees, is absolutely necessary if one is to go on looking and reflecting at all."[4]

Platonic in its guiding metaphor, Foucault's task at the juncture of **The Use of Pleasure** and **Le souci de soi**[5] is to engage in philosophy as the thought of the Other, the different, the alien, and what initiates thought by being the non-thought.

This shift in perspective is striking, since, up to the present, Foucault had avoided the use of the term, philosophy, in connection with his own efforts. In reassessing the direction of **The History of Sexuality**, and in responding to the life-crisis that the later two volumes represent, Foucault invokes philosophy as the rubric with which to cover his activity of self-critique and the critique of sexuality and morality. "But, then," he writes, "what is philosophy—philosophical activity, I mean— if it is not the critical work that thought brings to bear on itself: in what does it consist, if not in the endeavor to know how and to what extent it might be possible to think differently, instead of legitimating what is already known?"[6]

The analysis of "arts of existence" and "techniques of self" in **The Use of Pleasure** and **Le souci de soi** corresponds to a methodological counterpart: an *ascesis* on the part of philosophy, "an exercise of oneself in the activity of thought."[7] To the "problematization" of sexuality in the question of pleasure and in the relationship to self there is in **The Use of Pleasure** the problematization of the self as part of the discipline of the Other. Philosophy, in these efforts, loses much of what it has connoted in the secondary traditions of its history: abstractness, generality, formality, and apriority. Philosophy, in the context that Foucault's last works create for it, verges upon a concreteness and sensuality that the question of the use of pleasure broaches in the analysis of *aphrodisia*. If, in antiquity, the moral subject arises within the question of the use of pleasures, *aphrodisia*, then the subject of philosophy is constituted in the "essay" of thought to think what is different.

Clearly there is a difference here between the problem of *aphrodisia* and the question of philosophical *ascesis*, but there is a similarity in the mode or manner in which pleasure and philosophy are approached. Antiquity approached pleasure in terms of a relation to self, an art or aesthetics of existence. Foucault appears to have appropriated that discourse of his own as the practice of an exercise of the self in the activity of philosophy. This exercise is one of critique in which to rethink history is to bring into relief what was buried in the silence of the repressed and forgotten, yet formative, as the undertow of history, of what is thought.

Is this shift toward philosophy in **The Use of Pleasure** an abandonment of the theory of discursive practices and a taking shelter from the exposure to the infinity of language? Why philosophy? And why phrase the question in an existentialist manner, i.e., precipitated by a life crisis? Foucault implicitly answers those questions in **The Use of Pleasure** and **Le souci de soi**. The angle of approach of those later two volumes may not be congruent with the first volume of **The History of Sexuality**, but both sets of questions focus upon the same object: the desiring subject. Beneath the "affective mechanism of sexuality" of the first volume, Foucault uncovers the desiring subject, the self-consciousness that takes on form in the sexed body. It is the genealogy of that desiring subject that **The Use of Pleasure** and **Le souci de soi** prolongs by delineating the matrix in which antiquity embedded sexuality: in concern for the self in medicine and ethics and in the question of the use of *aphrodisia*. In the "arts of existence" which arise on the basis of the concern for self, the subject is posited as a moral subject for whom freedom from enslavement and control of self are the dominant values. The question of the use of pleasure and concern for self are, then, in turn, part of a larger question, i.e., the question of the constitution of the subject.

The question of the constitution of the subject as a formative part of the discourse of truth appears at the inception of Foucault's successive projects. From **Madness and Civilization**[8] to **The History of Sexuality**, the subject appears as the guilt subjectivized in the asylum, the gaze of clinical medicine, the site of discourse in institutions, man, the object of anthropological study, conceived in the analytic of finitude, and, finally, the individual, normalized and interiorized through the semiotechniques of penal discipline. For Foucault, however, the subject is not accessible through a description of lived experiences in which consciousness is face to face with itself and truth is marked by the clarity of presence. The subject is only accessible obliquely, not in the continuity of its self-consciousness, but in the discontinuity of its shifting forms, in the different interrogations to which it is submitted, and in the ways in which its interiority is hollowed out.

To what processes of subjectivization does the subject submit to become the subject of moral experiences? What is the process by which the subject becomes the moral subject? What is the subject of experiences? **The Use of Pleasure** and **Le souci de soi** come full cycle to rejoin some of the problematic engaged in **Madness and Civilization**, where, but in

Foucault's view, naively, the history of the asylum as formative of the perception of madness and the subject of madness as guilty consciousness was written as a history of experience. The contrast with the proposal in the "Introduction" to the **Will to Know**, the first volume of **The History of Sexuality**, is clear and explicit. In that volume, Foucault defined the object of his research as an analysis of sexuality in terms of the hypothesis of repression masking "a technology of power" and "a will to knowledge."[9]

"In short," Foucault writes, "I would like to disengage my analysis from the privileges generally accorded the economy of scarcity and the principles of rarefaction, to search instead for instances of discursive production (which sometimes have the function of prohibiting), of the propagation of knowledge (which often cause mistaken beliefs or systematic misconceptions to circulate); I would like to write the history of these instances and their transformation."[10] This program is deeply woven into the web of questions that surrounds the issue of power/knowledge. Knowledge as the technique of power, power as the elaboration of the field of knowledge, knowledge as domination of the object—issues that populate Foucault's works from **Madness and Civilization** to **The History of Sexuality**—are closely tied to the type of analysis that was developed in **The Archaeology of Knowledge**[11] and **The Order of Things**.[12] The description of discursive practices and their rules of formation focus upon the way that knowledge exists or is produced in the strategies, concepts, techniques and manipulations that objectify experiences by dominating the field of objectivity. But the theory of discursive practices is not philosophy. For archaeological and genealogical discourse, philosophy is a question; its objects are to be examined in their historical formation, i.e., the strategies that give rise to them. The concepts of philosophy are not foundational, but must be demystified by uncovering their genealogy and sifting through archaeological ruins. Nevertheless, where Foucault comes closest to the Heideggerian prophecy of the death of philosophy, he does not take up the Heideggerian theme. The death of man and the closure of the analytic of finitude with which **The Order of Things** ends is not a proclamation of the end of philosophy. It would seem that in Foucault's reticence about the fate of philosophy, there is involved the reticence of philosophy itself that does not allow itself to accompany its objects as they fall into the gaps that separate epistemological grids and epistemes.

Once the question of truth is broached through the problematization of the desiring subject in **The History of Sexuality**, then philosophy once agains comes into play. But philosophy comes into play by shifting the scene: the desiring subject and not the epistemological subject constitutive of its experiences provides the threshold for the question of truth. Philosophy becomes possible for Foucault on the basis of the appropriation of desire for the elaboration of a theory of the subject.

The crucial character of the appropriation of the subjectivity of desiring consciousness becomes apparent once one notices the issues that are raised in the midst of the description of the problematization of sexuality in antiquity and during the Empire. Sexuality is problematized in antiquity and during the Empire. Sexuality is problematized in antiquity on the basis of a relationship to self. **Madness and Civilization** highlighted the same process: the asylum ultimately created the subject of madness through the interiorization of moral guilt. That subjectivization made it possible to pose the question of reason and unreason. From that division, the work of art appears as the locus for the violence that in annihilating reason and the world shows their contours and limits and can move beyond reason by putting it into question.[13]

The discourse about the world and the language of reason which attempt to contain madness and explain it, rather than justifying madness, are justified by excesses to be found in those works (Van Gogh, Nietzsche, and Artaud) interrupted by the violence of madness/unreason. The truth of the world and the truth of reason do not lie, then, within the dialectic of reason, but in the void of the work of art in which reason and the world must answer the threat and the question of nothingness: "By the madness which interrupts it, a work of art opens a void, a moment of silence, a question without answer, provokes a breach without reconciliation where the world is forced to question itself."[14] The knowledge of reason by reason, the reflective moment in which reason begins to speak and to write, is constituted in the void exposed in the work of art through the savage violence of unreason. It is the contestation of the non-dialectical violence of madness/unreason that leads the world to question itself and to question itself in terms of its restoration and being.[15] Reason is born in the violence of the question posed to the world in the work of art: the world "is now arraigned by the work of art, obliged to order itself by its language, compelled by it to a task of recognition, or reparation, to the task of restoring reason **from** unreason and **to** that unreason."[16]

If it is, at a first glance, impossible to relate the question of the world raised upon the nothingness of the work of art to the question of the constitution of the moral subject in the use of pleasures, there is covert connection between them which

brings into relief the question of reason in its philosophical
dimensions as those circulate through the concept of truth. In
the volumes we presently have of **The History of Sexuality**,
the concept of truth as the "games of truth" approached very
cautiously the normativity of truth in relation to error. In these
volumes the history of truth is coupled to the history of ethics.
This is accomplished by means of the mediation of the concept
of the erotics of pleasure in which the relation to self is viewed
in terms of an "aesthetics" of existence. Foucault suggests
there a theme introduced in Nietzsche's **The Birth of Tragedy**
and recaptured in the thought of Heidegger: life as a work of
art; the work of art as the unconcealment of the world in the
struggle with the earth. For Foucault it is the substantive nature
of pleasure in its relation to the self in the thought of antiquity
which initiates the question of the aesthetics of reason and of
ethical reason. The normativity of truth is at once an aesthetical
and ethical question. The erotic raises, at the same time, the
question of truth in the context of social relations: self, the
other, friendship, men, women and boys.

At the conclusion of **The Use of Reason**, Foucault writes that
for the Greek "reflection on sexual behavior as a moral domain
was not a means of internalizing, justifying, or formalizing
general interdictions imposed on everyone: rather, it was a
means of developing—for the smallest minority of the population, made up of free, adult males—an aesthetics of existence, the purposeful art of a freedom perceived as a power
game."[17]

The ethics that is involved in the erotics of pleasure is not
concerned with the legitimacy of pleasures of actions in terms
of themselves, but of their use, of the style of life, active or
passive, dominant or subservient, virile or feminine, that involves pleasure. Posed in those terms, the intrinsic quality of
acts and corresponding pleasures do not form the substance
of the morality of sexuality, but, rather, that position is occupied by the role of the self in sexual behavior. The austere
use of pleasures stemmed from an ideal of moderation and
restraint in which the self was in control of itself, active, virile,
and dominant over others.

Through this problematization of sexuality as a question of
freedom the use of pleasures raises the question of truth. The
normative element of rationality enters into the discussion of
sexuality and the use of pleasures through the possibility of
the bondage of the self to pleasures and the enslavement of
freedom to its contrary: "This individual freedom should not,
however, be understood as the independence of a free will.
Its polar opposite was not a natural determinism, nor was it

the will of an all-powerful agency: it was enslavement—the enslavement of the self by oneself. To be free in relation to pleasures was to be free of their authority; it was not to be their slave."[18] This freedom embodied in austere moderation was a pre-condition for the correct use of political power, for in order to exercise power over others, it is necessary to be able to exercise control over oneself.

Foucault sees here a freedom to be found, not in independence from external influences, but a freedom to be found in praxis itself, in the doing of things that was part of the Greek sense of the political. To be free in doing things required that one was free with respect to the exercise of one's subjectivity. Sexual austerity thus required the development of a specific moral subject, one based on the exercise of virility in politics and the management of estates: "What one must aim for in the agonistic contest with oneself and in the struggle to control the desires was the point where the relationship with oneself would be isomorphic with the relationship of domination, hierarchy, and authority that one expected, as a man, a free man, to establish over his inferiors; and it was this prior condition of 'ethical virility' that provided one with the right sense of proportion for the exercise of 'sexual virility'."[19] For this subject, enslavement to pleasure was the opposite of activity, i.e., passivity. The pertinent question with respect to the use of pleasures was not what kind of pleasure was lawful, the love of women or the love of boys, but whether one was active or passive in the use of pleasure. In this manner, the moral subject of the art of living, as opposed to a subject formed in relation to universal moral laws, poses, in its problematization, the question of freedom and its exercise, not categories of actions and pleasures. The moral subject is a practical subject, the subjectivity of praxis, in which freedom demands the intervention of reason in determining its exercise. In this way, the question of sexuality raised in the use of pleasures is coupled with the question of the history of truth.

Freedom forces the issue of truth. Control over self and moderation are impossible without reason (*logos*). The praxis of freedom or moderation is impossible without knowledge. The very nature of praxis as a doing and exercise requires the intervention of reasoning; its non-intuitive character demands that one be able to discern the relation of the self to desires. **The Use of Pleasure** pinpoints three ways in which reason intervened in the practice of moderation: 1) a structural form: the subordination of desires and pleasures to reason, 2) an instrumental form: the use of pleasures in response to the right "needs, times, and circumstances," 3) an ontological form (Plato): "the ontological recognition of the self by the self."[20]

The requirements of practice, then, required that the moral subject also be the epistemological subject. In order to act, it was necessary to know. Correct practice or moderate practice depended upon reasons and a truth forged within the parameters of practice: truth arises from this struggle between acts, desires, and pleasures. From that struggle issues a mastery (*enkrateia*) over self in which moderation (*sophrosyne*) was the ideal. This mastery of self formed the ethical substance of the erotic of antiquity. It also exposes to view an aesthetics; not a series or set of laws to which the moral subject must submit, but a form of life in which an internal dynamics takes on a concrete shape out of the struggles with sensibility and out of the material of sensibility.

What makes it possible to pose the question of truth in the midst of the struggles of sensibility? Discourse does not function in **The Use of Pleasure** and **Le souci de soi** as the discursive practice in which truth as a system of exclusions is articulated. Rather, Foucault turns to a freedom that is based upon the interplay of differences, a curiosity, or desire to know that is motivated and captured by differences. Freedom is to think differently than what one already knows. It is the freedom of philosophy to be anti-philosophy, i.e., to critique the presuppositions and exclusions of thought in order to clear space for the question. The freedom of thought which initiates and sustains critique is the contestation of the difference, the transgression of limits which destroys the illusion of identity in sameness.

The History of Sexuality raises the question of the origin and normativity of truth on the basis of the pre-conditions of discourse as discursive practice, semio-technique, and the interplay of power/knowledge. The normativity of truth is a question posed to practice by the rationality of practice, practical reason. The excess of what is desired over what is natural creates a lack of convergence within sensibility itself: pleasure is disproportionate to itself. It is not its own norm in practice. Practical reason installs itself in that excess.[21] The norm of practical reason is installed in the difference that separates pleasure from itself: its inability to norm itself and to encounter its own limits outside of practice.

Philosophy returns to the writings of Foucault, consequently, in a strange guise: the freedom arising from the excess of sensibility. The disproportionality at the heart of pleasures demands a practical resolution. The form that resolution takes is not the drawing of limits around pleasures, but the self-limiting practice of moderation. But moderation is a limit without limits; it cannot by its nature prescribe rules. It must rely

garth gillan

on the freedom of an excess to measure and weigh its choices. A constantly shifting limit, moderation and the thought that moves within its dynamic is always haunted by its opposite: excess. Hence at the foundations of philosophy we encounter a freedom made possible by an anti-freedom, a philosophy driven by the specter of anti-philosophy, and a subject living in fear of the anti-subject.

Subtly **The History of Sexuality** is restoring to philosophy the *agon*, the struggle of thought with itself. In the space of excess, philosophy is the contest of opposites. From that contest truth issues as the result of a freedom on the brink, always this side of what will pull it under. Beneath the will to know there is an erotics of knowledge. Practical rationality spans the difference in desire. The fragility of that practice issuing from the contradictions of desire is another name for the truth.

We think more honestly after Foucault.

Southern Illinois University

NOTES

1. Hubert L. Dreyfus and Paul Rabinow, **Michel Foucault, Beyond Structuralism and Hermeneutics** (Chicago: University of Chicago Press, 1982); Mark Cousins and Athar Hussain, **Michel Foucault** (New York: St. Martin's Press, 1984).

2. Michel Foucault, **The Use of Pleasure** (New York: Pantheon Books, 1985).

3. **Ibid.**, 8.

4. **Ibid.**

5. Michel Foucault, **Le souci de soi, Histoire de la sexualité**, vol. 3, (Paris: Editions Gallimard, 1984)

6. **The Use of Pleasure**, p. 9

7. **Ibid.**

8. Michel Foucault, **Madness and Civilization** (New York: New American Library, 1967).

9. Michel Foucault, **The History of Sexuality, Volume I: An Introduction** (New York: Random House, 1980), p. 12.

10. **Ibid.**

11. Michel Foucault, **The Archaeology of Knowledge**, trans. A.M. Sheridan Smith (New York: Harper Colophon, 1972).

12. Michel Foucault, **The Order of Things: An Archaeology of The Human Sciences** (New York: Random House, 1973).

13. **Madness and Civilization**, p. 230.

14. **Ibid.**

43

15. **Ibid.**, p. 231

16. **Ibid.**

17. **The Use of Pleasure**, p. 252–3

18. **Ibid.**, p. 79

19. **Ibid.**, p. 83

20. **Ibid.**, p. 86–88

21. **Ibid.**, p. 43.

james w. bernauer

michel foucault's ecstatic thinking

Although Michel Foucault's life was cut short by a premature death, his work was not deprived of a good measure of completion. His published writings span a period of thirty years and, while they manifest an extraordinary range of interests, there is a remarkable coherence to the achievement of a philosopher who was so willfully anti-systematic. The key to that coherence, however, is to be found neither in the particular topics he investigated nor in the different methods he pursued. Running through these, amid the scattered researches on one hand and the refining of method on the other, was a fundamental interrogation of his experience of thinking itself, a continuing concern with the route it should follow if research was to be more than academic exercise and method more potent than arrangement of material. The single experience which was always at the source of his thought was the reality of imprisonment, the incarceration of human beings within modern systems of thought and practice which had become so intimately a part of them that they no longer experienced these systems as a series of confinements but embraced them as the very structure of being human. The prison of modern humanism which incited his thought was not just the intellectual confinement constructed by a-historical views of human nature and the egocentric illusions of modern subjectivity; it was also a moral confinement for within this prison "reason ceased to be for man an ethic and became a nature."[1] Although an explicit consideration of ethics awaited his last writings, Foucault's history of knowledge-power relations implicitly struggled against this reduction of reason to nature.

Many of Foucault's critics accused him not only of identifying confinements but of celebrating them, of producing such a feeling of entrapment about the ways we act and think that his readers were left with no scope for personal freedom and no hope for significant political or cultural change. That, of course, was neither his intention nor, I would maintain, his accomplishment. If imprisonment was the experience which provoked Foucault's research and reflection, it was the winding path of his thought which attempted to exhibit the routes of escape. After his history of madness shattered the initial project which had harbored his thought, namely, the search for a true psychology of man, Foucault's work forged a series of distinct experiences of thinking as well as operations for the conduct of inquiry.[2] Four experiences define the basic stages in his intellectual journey and the fundamental operations of archaeological-genealogical inquiry. The first of them, represented best in **The Order of Things**, was a cathartic thinking, the effort to comprehend and purge the epistemic conditions determining the major principles of current knowledge in the sciences of man. This need for catharsis was personal, for an archaeology of the human sciences would reveal to Foucault why the question of man formed the ground of his first philosophical project; in doing that, such a catharsis would also excavate the roots of both modern anthropological concern in general and its major forms of inquiry, hermeneutics and structuralism. This exposure of major epistemic strata in the emergence of the human sciences was performed for the sake of "restoring to our silent and apparently immobile soil its rifts, its instability, its flaws."[3] In the methodological concentration of 1969 to 1971, Foucault portrays a thinking which has been liberated from the anthropological theme and which defines its analysis as neither interpretation nor formalization. Archaeology is put forward as a thinking which aims at the emancipation of dissonance, the exposure of thought to reality as a multiplicity of events which stand in need of new, non-dialectical orderings.[4] The objective of his work is to develop a thinking adequate to events and, thus, permit the "introduction into the very roots of thought, of notions of chance, discontinuity and materiality."[5] From 1972 to 1979, Foucault was engaged in an archaeology-genealogy of politics, a task which manifested itself in a dissident thinking, a continuing challenge to the forms of power's practice in our society, and to the types of understanding which hide the grounds for these forms. His dissident thinking was no less cathartic or dissonant, but its uncovering of foundations was now welded to explicitly political tasks.[6] All of these Foucaultian experiences of thought denature or historicize Kant's great questions. Not "What can I know?," but rather, "How have my questions been produced? How has the path of my knowing been determined?" Not "What ought I to do?," but rather, "How have I been situated to experience the real? How have exclusions operated in delineating the realm of obligation for me?'' Not "What may I hope for?," but rather, "What are the struggles in which I am engaged? How have the parameters for my aspirations been defined?"

The last experience of thought which Foucault elaborated as an escape from the prison of humanism was an ecstatic thinking, a characterization which may be understood provisionally as a designation for two transitions. First, it acknowledges a double movement of his thought in his last works: a transition both to issues of ethical subjectivity and individual conduct as well as a transfer of research from the modern period to the classical and early Christian eras. The occasion for this shift was his study of Christian experience. The first section of this essay, On Christian Experience, focuses on the context and content of this study, which would have been the substance of the announced fourth volume in his history of sexuality, **Confessions of the Flesh**. In respect of Foucault's own wishes, this unfinished volume may never appear. It is my hope that even a brief review of his insights into Christianity will give a clearer understanding of why Foucault's final work evolved in the way that it did. The second and more important dimension constituting Foucault's ecstatic thinking is his effort to pass beyond the modern mode of being a subject. This movement will be the focal point for the essay's next two sections. The Politics of Our Selves delineates Foucault's archaeology of the Freudian hermeneutical subject; this Freudian subject exemplified the modern form of relating to the self. This archaeology was the precondition for the ecstatic thinking which will be explicitly treated in our third section. It explores the experience of thinking which makes comprehensible the strange maxim at which Foucault's path concluded, his counsel to get free of oneself. In the conclusion, we suggest a synoptic viewpoint on Foucault's achievement, his diagram for an ethics of thought.

It is the unusual character both of ecstatic thinking and its maxim which accounts for some of the harsh responses which have marked the reception for Foucault's last writings. Two recent voices may be cited as representative of this large chorus of critics. Maria Daraki writes of his study on Greek ethics: "It is not a question of 'errors' of scholarship. Foucault is a hard-working and well-informed writer. It is, rather, a question of this tragic blindness the Greeks called Ate which takes hold of a man like a daimon. Foucault's daimon is a fantasm of dominating narcissism which demands the sacrifice of all facts." Richard Wolin argues that "Foucault's position ultimately becomes indistinguishable from that of a narcissistic child who deems 'maturity' in all its forms simply repressive."[7]

What are we to make of such a style of criticism? Having wondered for several years about the violent reactions Foucault evokes, I have come to conclude that his work, especially its last stage, scraped an especially sensitive area of contemporary consciousness, not only its reluctance to think differently, but more importantly, its sacrilization of the modern experience of the self. This experience functions as a refuge from a world and history that are grasped as fatally determined. Foucault's uncovering of the early processes from which the experience of the self derives, and his call to abandon that experience, affronted not only a philosophical position but a love, a self-love which survives in a culture which has lost its way intellectually, politically and morally. The charges of narcissism against a thinker who proclaims the need for a freedom from our current relations to the self are a subterfuge meant to conceal a narcissistic attachment to an experience of the person, which Foucault's entire work attempted to subvert. If his earlier declaration of the "death of man" was tolerable, it is because it was directed at forces which could still be considered as somehow extrinsic to the self; the ecstatic renunciation of the modern relation to the self, which is announced in Foucault's last writings, was unacceptable, because all too many in his audience have only that relation as an imagined last barrier to nihilism.

1. On Christian Experience

While there had been scattered remarks on Christian themes in his earlier studies, it was only with his investigation of normalization and sexuality that Christian experience became an explicit focus of Foucault's work. At first, this focus was totally subordinated to other interests. His 1975 course at the Collège, which was a transition from the study of the prison, sought to grasp how the general domain of abnormality was opened up for a psychiatric understanding. Foucault laid responsibility for this development on the articulation of sexuality as a dimension within all abnormality and, most importantly, on the necessity for each individual to avow a sexual identity. His effort to analyze the conditions accounting for the appearance of this obligatory avowal of sexuality encouraged him to study the Christian practice of confession. Confession was a topic which Ivan Illich had once recommended to him for examination, and which Foucault had mentioned in his inaugural address at the Collège in the context of a possible investigation of its role in the functioning of the "taboo system" involved with the language of sexuality.[8] Neither his 1975 course nor the first volume of his history of sexuality entailed a turn from modernity itself as Foucault's field of interest. His initial james bernauer examination of confession concentrated on its practice after the Council of Trent (1545–1563) and the expansion of this "millennial yoke of confession" to ever larger numbers of relationships in the period after the Reformation.[9] Despite this modern perspective, Foucault came to the insight which would motivate a more intense study of Christian writers and, ultimately, of ethical self-formation: "Now we must ask what happened in the sixteenth century. The period which is characterized not by the beginning of a dechristianization but by the beginning of a christianization-in-depth."[10]

It was a very circuitous route that led him to an investigation of early Christianity's experience of the subject, a route barely suggested by Foucault's own accounts.[11] Foucault first sketched the plan of a multi-volume history of sexuality in the context of an analysis of modern bio-politics, which designated those forces which "brought life and its mechanisms into the realm of explicit calculations and made knowledge-power an agent of transformation of human life."[12] In the emergence of this bio-politics, sexuality was a crucial domain because it was located at the pivot of the two axes along which Foucault saw the power over life developing: access both to the individual body and the social body.[13]

The titles of the projected volumes in the series on sexuality indicated the direction he intended to pursue in exploring the constitution of modern "sexuality." The planned second volume, **Flesh and Body**, would have sketched the difference between a premodern approach to sexual experience, as a realm of necessary religious and moral asceticism, developed in relation to a juridical code, and the modern fabrication of sexuality as a domain of knowledge-power centered on the body. The succeeding volumes would take up each of the major nineteenth century sexual unities that were the principal vehicles for knowledge-power relations to operate. Volume 3, **The Children's Crusade,** would treat how children were sexualized and how their sexual behavior became a major concern for education. Volume 4, **Woman, Mother and Hysteric**, would study the sexualization of the woman's body, the concepts of pathology which arose in relation to that sexualization, and the insertion of that body into a perspective which invested it with significance for social policy. Volume 5, **Perverts**, would study the isolation of sex as an instinct, the definition of its normal and abnormal functioning, and the corrective technology envisioned to deal with the latter. Volume 6, **Population and Races**, would examine how the sexual domain became an object for ever increasing state intervention, as well as the emergence of eugenics and theories of race in the contemporary configuration of knowledge.[14]

In the years immediately after the publication of the history of sexuality's introductory volume, Foucault's research roamed across a field of topics closely related to the issues of the projected last volume. In 1976, he taught a course on the appearance of a discourse on war and how it functioned as an analysis of social relations; in 1978 and 1979, he presented courses on the genesis of a political rationality which placed the notion of population and the mechanisms to assure its regulation at the center of its concern, and he conducted seminars on the theory of police science and on the juridical thought of the nineteenth century.[15]

Despite the variety, however, a special concern took shape which oriented Foucault's approach to the study of Christianity. He became preoccupied with the problematic of governance which appeared in the sixteenth century and which showed itself in the development and dissemination of discourses on personal conduct, on the art of directing souls, and on the manner of educating children. This intensified Foucault's exploration of the crisis of the Reformation and Counter-Reformation, which entailed an anxiety over the matter of governance by putting in "question the manner in which one is to be spiritually ruled and led on this earth to achieve eternal salvation."[16] The exploration of the knowledge-power relations involved by governance directed him to an analysis of the Christian pastorate and, thus, to confrontation with the ethical formation critical to its way of obtaining knowledge and exercising power.

The first major statement of the results of his research in premodern Christian experience came with his course, "On the Governance of the Living," which he presented in 1980. The prelude for this course was his series of two lectures at Stanford University in late 1979, and its discoveries were refined in later courses, lectures and publications.[17]

Foucault's reading of the Christian experience was selective, but it was decisive in expanding his horizon beyond modernity and especially beyond power-knowledge relations to an inclusion of subjectivity. In his 1980 course, Foucault presented this new regime against the background of an opening meditation on Sophocle's **Oedipus**, in which he followed the objective construction of the King's true identity by the authorized voices of others, voices which terminated the search for truth. Christianity put forward a far different search, one which embraced different forms of power, knowledge and relation to self. It is the continuing vitality of variations of each of these which justifies Foucault's claim of a "christianization-in-depth" throughout the modern period.

james bernauer **Power**. Christian experience represents the development of a new form of individualizing power, that of the pastorate, which has its roots in the Hebraic image of God and his deputed King as shepherds. This power is productive, not repressive. Exercising authority over a flock of dispersed individuals rather than a land, the shepherd has the duty to guide his charges to salvation by means of a continuous watch over them and a permanent concern with their well-being as individuals. Christianity intensifies this concern by having the pastors assume a responsibility for all the good and evil done by those for whom they are accountable and whose actions reflect upon their quality as shepherds.[18] Paramount in the exercise of this pastoral power is a virtue of obedience in the subject, a virtue which becomes an end in itself. "It is a permanent state; the sheep must permanently submit to their pastors: *subditi*. As Saint Benedict says, monks do not live according to their own free will; their wish is to be under the abbot's command."[19] Such obedience is the necessary antidote to the condition of the human being after Adam's Fall. With the Fall, the original subordination which human nature accorded to soul and will was lost, and the human being became a figure of revolt not only against God but also against himself. This situation was graphically illustrated in the lawlessness of the sexual yearnings.

The famous gesture of Adam covering his genitals with a fig leaf is, according to Augustine, not due to the simple fact that Adam was ashamed of their presence, but to the fact that his sexual organs were moving by themselves without his consent. Sex in erection is the image of man revolted against God. The arrogance of sex is the punishment and consequence of the arrogance of man. His uncontrolled sex is exactly the same as what he himself has been toward God—a rebel.[20]

This seditious sexuality signals the need for a struggle with one's self, and permanent obedience is essential to this struggle. The obedience which is intrinsic to the exercise and responsibilities of pastoral power involves specific forms of knowledge and of subjectivity.

Knowledge. In order to fulfill the responsibility of directing souls to their salvation, the pastor must understand the truth, not just the general truths of faith but the specific truths of each person's soul. For Foucault, Christianity is unique in the major truth obligations which are imposed upon its followers. In addition to accepting moral and dogmatic truths, they must also become excavators of their own personal truth: "Everyone in Christianity has the duty to explore who he is, what is happening within himself, the faults he may have committed, the temptations to which is he exposed."[21] Perhaps the most dramatic illustration of this obligation to discover and manifest one's truth took place in those liturgical ceremonies in which the early Christians would avow their state as sinners and then take on the status of public penitents.[22] Less dramatic but more enduring was the search for truth served by those practices of examination of conscience and confession which Christianity first developed in monastic life. This search entailed a permanent struggle with the Evil One who "hides behind seeming likenesses of oneself" and whose mode of action in the person is error.[23] The Christian campaign for self-knowledge was not directly developed in the interest of controlling sexual conduct but rather for the sake of a deepened awareness of one's interior life. "Cassian is interested in the movements of the body and the mind, images, feelings, memories, faces in dreams, the spontaneous movements of thoughts, the consenting (or refusing) will, waking and sleeping."[24] Foucault was fond of citing three comparisons which Cassian employed to portray the process of spiritual self-scrutiny. It is compared with the work of a miller who must sort out the good and bad grains before admitting them to the millstone of thought; another likens it to the responsibility of a centurion who must evaluate his soldiers in order to assign them to their proper tasks; finally, one must be like a money-changer who studies the coins presented to him in order to judge those which are authentic from those which are not.[25] All of these affirm the rigorous self-analysis to which Christian practice was committed as well as anticipate modern recourse to a hermeneutics of suspicion. In addition, this endless task of self-doubt is accompanied by regular confessions to another, for verbalization of thoughts is another level of sorting out the good thoughts from those which are evil, namely, those which seek to hide from the light of public expression.[26] By means of its examination of conscience and confession, Christianity fashions a technology of the self which enabled people to transform themselves.[27] The principal production of this technology was a unique form of subjectivity.

Subjectivity. Within Christianity, there has taken place an interiorization or subjectivization of the human being, an event which Foucault locates as the outcome of two processes. The first is the constitution of the self as a hermeneutical reality, namely, the recognition that there is a truth in the subject, that the soul is the place where this truth resides, and that true discourses are able to be articulated concerning it.[28] The Christian self is an obscure text demanding permanent interpretation through ever more sophisticated practices of attentiveness, concern, decipherment and verbalization. The second james bernauer process is one which is both paradoxical and yet essential for appreciating the unique mode of Christian subjectivity. The deciphering of one's soul is but one dimension of the subjectivity which relates the self to the self. While it involves an "indeterminate objectivization of the self by the self-indeterminate in the sense that one must be forever extending as far as possible the range of one's thoughts, however insignificant and innocent they may appear to be," the point of such objectivization is not to assemble a progressive knowledge of oneself for the sake of achieving the self-mastery which classical pagan thought advanced as an ideal.[29] The purpose of the Christian hermeneutic of the self is to foster renunciation of the self who has been objectified. The individual's relation to the self imitates both the baptismal turning from the old self who one was to a newly found otherness, as well as the ceremony of public penance that was depicted as a form of martyrdom which proclaimed the symbolic death of who one had been. The continual mortification entailed by a permanent hermeneutic and renunciation of the self makes of that symbolic death an everyday event. All truth about the self is tied to the sacrifice of that same self and the Christian experience of subjectivity declares itself most clearly in the sounds of a rupture with oneself, of an admission that "I am not who I am."[30] This capacity for self-renunciation was built from the ascetical power with regard to oneself, which was generated by a practice of obedience, and from the scepticism with respect to one's knowledge of oneself, which was created by hermeneutical self-analysis. Foucault's interpretation of Christian experience and his recognition of these two processes decisively shaped the major themes and interests of his last work: first, his project of an historical ontology of ourselves with its genealogy of the man of desire; secondly, his vision of a contemporary philosophical ethos. These form the substance of our next two sections.

2. The Politics of Our Selves

Foucault's first volume of the history of sexuality, with its recognition of bio-politics, already appreciated the key role which sexuality exercises in the modern deployment of power-knowledge. The most graphic example he gave of how this power operated for an individual was found in the memoirs of a nineteenth-century hermaphrodite, Herculine Barbin, a document which Foucault published in 1978 and on which he wrote an essay two years later.[31] Upon her birth in 1838, Barbin was baptized as a girl and lived with that status for the next twenty years. At that time, however, she found herself subjected to new and precise categories of a single, true sexual identity with the result that a civil court decreed a change of gender status and of name for her; on June 22, 1860, Mademoiselle Herculine became Monsieur Abel. Although the local newspapers carried sensational reports on her small town's reaction to the shocking transformation of its school-mistress, they were generally sympathetic to her plight for, as the papers pointed out, she had "lived piously and modestly until today in ignorance of herself."[32] Despite the sympathy, it can hardly come as a surprise that, eight years later, his-her corpse was discovered, a suicide or, rather, to Foucault's mind, the victim of a new passion for the truth of sexual identity.

And yet not totally new. In the light of his study of Christianity, Foucault saw that Barbin's fate was tied to a "demonic" transformation of that Christian pastorship whose elements are "life, death, truth, obedience, individuals, self-identity."[33] Far from diminishing with the decline of its ecclesiastical in-stitutionalization, pastoral power spread and multiplied within the modern state, which may itself be understood as a "new form of pastoral power."[34] Although its aims may have become worldly, the effect of state power is to mold a precise kind of individuality with which one's desire is incited to identify. If sexuality is most often the "seismograph" of that identity, it is because the legacy of the Christian technology of the self is to have linked "sexuality, subjectivity and truth" together as the terrain for self-discovery.[35] Foucault's realization of that triad's existence had two immediate effects on the way he articulated his own project. First, he particularized political struggle in terms of what he called a "politics of our selves."[36] In addition to resistance against forms of domination and types of exploitation, politics necessarily entails combat with a pas-toral power which "categorizes the individual, marks him by his own individuality, attaches him to his own identity, imposes a law of truth on him which he must recognize" and which "makes individuals subjects." Because of the pastoral func-tioning of state power, present political struggles must "re-volve around the question: Who are we? They are a refusal of these abstractions, of economic and ideological state vio-lence which ignores who we are individually, and also a refusal of a scientific or administrative inquisition which determines who one is." If one side of this resistance is to "refuse what we are," the other side is to invent, and not discover, who we are by promoting "new forms of subjectivity."[37] The second effect on Foucault's articulation of the project derives from the first. It is because he conceives of the political issue as a politics of our selves that the practice of ethics becomes central to his last work, an ethics "understood as the elaboration of a form of relation to self that enables an individual to fashion himself into a subject of ethical conduct.''[38] It does not represent an abandonment of his interest in politics, but, rather, is an effort to get at a form of becoming a subject which would furnish the source of an effective resistance to a specific and widespread type of power. This is why he was able to speak of his final concerns in terms of ''politics as an ethics.''[39] The prelude to the practice of an ethics which is politically effective is a defamiliarization of the ''desiring man'' who lies at the root of our willingness to identify with the form of individual subjectivity constructed for us in the modern period. Thus, one of the central enterprises of the second and third volumes in his history of sexuality was to ''investigate how individuals were led to practice, on themselves and on others, a hermeneutics of desire,'' and to ''analyze the practices by which individuals were led to focus their attention on themselves, to decipher, recognize, and acknowledge themselves as subjects of desire, bringing into play between themselves and themselves a certain relationship that allows them to discover, in desire, the truth of their being, be it natural or fallen.''[40] Such a project is an ''historical ontology of ourselves,'' an investigation of how we have been fashioned as ethical subjects. While the domain of such a study is ethics, its aim is to sustain a form of resistance to newly recognized political forces.[41]

The significance and form of Foucault's history of the man of desire is best grasped if it is understood in the context of its contribution to his ''archaeology of psychoanalysis''; the objective of this latter project was to undermine modern anthropology and the notion of the self which was one of its firmest supports and expressions.[42]

Freud's understanding is a model of this notion, and, thus, becomes the principal target of Foucault's effort to render the self freshly problematic. The failure to recognize the confrontation with Freud that is taking place in Foucault's last works has often prevented commentators from appreciating his intentions and organization in these writings, most especially, with regard to their central history of the man of desire. Foucault's dialogue with Freud and psychoanalysis continued throughout his career. In the context of his account of how madness was reduced to the empty, inauthentic speech of mental illness in the modern asylum and in psychiatry, Foucault nevertheless acknowledges Freud's greatest achievement. Freud's work brought the ''violence of a return'' for, in place of the asylum's cult of observation, he returned to madness at the level of its language, so radically different from everyday speech. He was the ''first to undertake the radical erasure of the division between . . . the normal and the pathological, the comprehensible and the communicable, the significant and the non-significant.'' Freud's accomplishment and, thus, his "scandal" for psychology and psychiatry was his challenge to their anthropology, their grasp of human being as a "homo psychologicus" who was positive in his self-consciousness.[43] In the first volume of his later history of sexuality, Foucault paid tribute to the opposition which psychoanalysis maintained against the "political and institutional effects of the perversion-heredity- degenerescence system" that was allied with a state-directed racism.[44] Despite these achievements, however, Freud and psychoanalysis remain exemplary of the system from which Foucault sought escape. Taking Foucault's own mention of Sophocles's **Oedipus** in his 1980 course as a clue, I wish to indicate how his history of the man of desire is the last stage in his subversion of the psychoanalytic vision of the person.

Freud's interpretation of the play is familiar. For him, Oedipus's search for the truth "can be likened to the work of a psychoanalysis." One relentlessly pursues the truth of one's identity, which is hidden far from one's conscious awareness and which shows itself as tied to the dimension of desire and sexuality. The story possesses perennial appeal because we recognize ourselves in Oedipus. As Freud points out: "His destiny moves us—because the oracle laid the same curse upon us before our birth as upon him."[45] Perhaps the myth would attract Foucault because it portrays so well the major domains of his own work: an analysis of the knowledges through which we are constructed as knowable and from which we derive the paths for fleeing self-ignorance; an examination of the power relations generated with those knowledges and of the systems of dependence to which we become subject in seeking our truth; finally, a study of how subjectivity became intimately associated with both truth and sexuality, how the discovery of one's true sex is the discovery of one's true self. In Foucault's earlier writing, the archaeology of psychoanalysis involved an identification of its general power—knowledge relations, especially its relationship to a medical model and its notion of the unconscious; in the first volume of his history of sexuality, it entailed a critique of the place psychoanalysis occupies in the modern deployment of sexuality; finally, his history of the man of desire excavates the relationship of the self to the self which operates in Freudian thought. I shall touch on the first two stages with brevity.

While Freud admitted that psychoanalysis "had its origin on medical soil," he had hoped that it could be transplanted.[46] Foucault's **The Birth of the Clinic** indicated, however, that modern readings of the person are tied to a medical perception. The work argued that clinical medicine was the first science of the individual. Integral to this science was the role of death as constitutive of one's individuality and unique intelligibility, a status which was the precondition for the extraordinary importance given by historians to pathological anatomy in the development of a science of medicine. Death and disease broke from metaphysical understandings and became essential elements in the identity of the person. The idea of a disease attacking life and destroying it is replaced by the conception that death is embodied in the living bodies of individuals. It is not because diseases attack him that man dies; it is because he will die that he is susceptible to disease. Created here was the crucially significant notion of a "pathological life" which can be carefully chartered and analyzed in terms of an **individual's** existence. But death is the essential truth of human life and any inquiry into the meaning of individual life is guaranteed to meet that medical perception which holds up to man the "face of his finitude," but which also promises to exorcise it through certain techniques.[47] The medical component is clear in questions of sexuality but, if Foucault is correct, all knowledge of the modern finite, bound-to-death self is oriented, by its very object, to aim at a truth which aspires to function as cure. This would account for why Freud, who could demystify so many of the asylum's major structures—its constant silence, observation, condemnation—could not eliminate the place which the doctor occupied and upon whom these transformed structures were concentrated: the trained observer whose silence is judgment. It is the very knowledge of our finite, individual selves which invites a medical paradigm and which accounts for the fact that, in our culture, Freud and medical thought have come to take on philosophical significance.[48] The controversies which swirl around the relationship between medicine and psychoanalysis are native and permanent to Freudian thought to the extent of its modernity. Foucault's **The Order of Things** extended his archaeology of psychoanalysis by indicating the foundations for the specific character of the unconscious which is at the core of psychoanalytic self-knowledge. Psychoanalysis occupies a central position in modern thought because it explores, but is also defined by, an opaqueness or unconsciousness generated by modern knowledge's dispersion of man within processes of life, labor and language. All of these possess histories alien to and independent of man. The themes of Death, Desire and Law, in which one's psychoanalytic search for intelligibility takes place, are born together with and remain dependent upon modern knowledge's drawing of man in those great colors of life, labor, speech. In exploring these psychoanalytic themes, western culture is brought back to the foundations for its anthropological knowledge and, thus, as Foucault points out, "pivots on the work of Freud, though without, for all that, leaving its fundamental arrangement."[49]

The central role which sexuality plays in the psychoanalytic image of the person is the next major element which indicates Freudian thought's coherence with the modern network of knowledge-power. Psychoanalysis is in alliance with the modern period's threefold sexual production: the creation of sexuality as a reality, especially the sexualization of children's experience; the constitution of a *scientia sexualis* based on global study of the population and analytic study of the individual; the privileging of sexuality as the access to the truth of human identity. The "cultural vigor" of psychoanalysis is at the "junction of these two ideas—that we must not deceive ourselves concerning our sex, and that our sex harbors what is most true in ourselves."[50] Despite its greater subtlety, psychoanalysis operates within the modern regime of sexuality and even intensifies it. It gives support to the conception of sex as a stubborn drive, constantly at war with repressive powers; psychoanalysis, therefore, obscures the positive function of power as productive of what we take the sexual realm and its themes to be. And, for Foucault, this is the case whether the psychoanalytic approach is according to a theory of instincts or in terms of how the law itself constitutes the nature of sexual desire. In addition, psychoanalysis unifies the system of the family with the modern sphere of sexuality by placing the incest desire at the center of the individual's sexual life. Freud cooperates in constituting the family as a privileged target for political governance in that it is transformed into the "germ of all the misfortunes of sex." Finally, psychoanalysis provides one of the most striking examples in the modern transformation of pastoral power. It has taken over the techniques of confessional practice and, thus, places the individual under the obligation to manifest truth to another in a situation of dependence and through the action of speech, which is invested with a special virtue of verification.[51]

The greatest support for the psychoanalytic project is provided by a special relationship which the self takes up with itself, namely, that sexuality is the index of one's subjectivity, of one's true self. The kinship of subjectivity-truth-sexuality is the lynchpin of Freudian thought. The capacity of sexual desires and deeds to become the most revealing signs of our truest, deepest selves is dependent upon a long historical formation through which we were created as subjects in a special relation to both truth and sex. I have already indicated that their actual historical fusion is, for Foucault, a legacy of Christian experience. That experience, however, is the last of the three moments in early Western culture's constitution of this kinship. Foucault's final two volumes study the first two moments in the construction of western subjectivity, the cultures of classical Greece and the later Graeco-Roman period. The initial interrogation of the "man of desire" grew from the soil of Greek ethics. The central problematic of this pre-Platonic ethic was the proper use of pleasures so that one could achieve the mastery over oneself which made one fit to be a free citizen and worthy to exercise authority over others. Each of the great arts of Greek conduct of the self involved with sexual matters— dietetics, economics, and erotics—was characterized by a program of moderation. Dietetics directed a moderation which recognized the special anxiety provoked by the use of sexual pleasures, pleasures which were experienced as perilous because they entailed violence to the body and encounter with death as well as the transmission of life. Economics guided a man's training in self-mastery by regulating the conduct with his wife in the interest of the hierarchial structure appropriate to the sphere of the household.[52] Foucault exposes the earliest pre-history of modern subjectivity in his consideration of erotics, the Greek art of love.

At the center of this art was the special relationship in that culture between the older male, who was an active participant in the city, and the young male, who was still dependent upon others for his educational formation. While sexual relations between the two were fully accepted, this acceptance was not at all a simple matter, and Foucault points to much evidence which indicates a persistent uneasiness about the relationship: an oscillation in its regard between what was thought natural or unnatural; a clear reticence to speak about these sexual relations as well as a reluctance to concede that the younger male might experience pleasure through them; the relationship was also explicitly subordinated to the non-sexual friendship which should be its eventual outcome.[53] The complexity of Greek erotics is partially due to the fact that, unlike dietetics and economics, in which a man's moderation was rooted in his relationship to himself, the love between the older and younger male implied a moderation by both and the alliance of these moderations in a mutual respect for the other's freedom. The principal source of the relationship's complexity, and of the elaborate courtship practice and moral reflection which surrounded it, was what Foucault describes as the problem of the "antinomy of the boy" in the Greek ethics of the use of pleasure.[54]

While adolescent boys were recognized as legitimate objects of pleasure, their youth was also a trial period in which they learned the dishonor of conducting themselves passively. The adolescent free male was expected to train himself to assume his freedom through an exercise of self-contol in order to prove his capability of governing others. Sexual relations were conceived in terms of the fundamental act as penetration and so were regarded as exhibiting a polarity between positively valued active and negatively viewed passive forms of conduct. Inasmuch as there was an isomorphism between sexual and political relations, the youth's training in the conduct appropriate for a free, active citizen was morally at variance with any relationship which would make him a passive object of pleasure: "But while the boy, because of his peculiar charm, could be a prey that men might pursue without causing a scandal or a problem, one had to keep in mind that the day would come when he would have to be a man, to exercise powers and responsibilities, so that obviously he could then no longer be an object of pleasure—but then, to what extent could he **have been** such an object?"[55]

It is clear that the moral preoccupation of the Greeks with this relationship interrogated neither the nature nor the subject of the desire which inclined an individual to the relationship. The movement to that form of questioning came only with the Socratic-Platonic reflection on love itself which endeavored to resolve the problematic of the antinomy of the boy. The ethic of the use of pleasure involved a form of knowledge which guided a person's moderation, either in terms of a structural form of knowledge, which declared the supremacy of reason over desire, or in terms of an instrumental form of knowledge which gave practical directions for using pleasure. With Plato, however, a third form of knowledge is introduced, the "need to know oneself in order to practice virtue and subdue the desires." Foucault calls this the "ontological recognition of the self by the self," which represents a new rapport between truth and the self.[56] What creates this rapport and the displacement of the moral problematic of male courtship by a preoccupation with truth and the effort to achieve it is a series of philosophical transformations, to which Plato's **Symposium** and **Phaedrus** give witness. There is a transformation of the earlier culture's deontological question about what is proper conduct by an ontological investigation into the very nature and origin of love. Questions about the one who is loved are replaced by those which inquire about the one who loves and what he knows about the being of love. A second transformation is from a concern with the honor of the boy to the issue of the lover's love for the truth which enables him to distinguish the good from the bad forms of love. Thirdly, there is a shift from the difficult moral problem posed by a dissymmetry of partners to the notion of a convergence in a true love which transcends and draws them: "unlike what occurs in the art of courtship, the 'dialectic of love' in this case calls for two move-ments exactly alike on the part of the two lovers; the love is the same for both of them, since it is the motion which carries them toward truth."[57] Finally, inasmuch as *eros* is drawn to the true, it is the one who has moved farthest on the road toward truth who becomes the central figure in the love re-lationship. A dramatic reversal takes place: the master of truth comes to take the place of the lover, and the love of the master, as in the relationship of youths to Socrates, becomes dominant over the previous concern with the virtue of the boy.

While this philosophical erotics emerged from the problematic of the earlier Greek ethic, it also signals a major step beyond it. The soul's effort to progress in truth and love demands a novel interrogation about the being of its desire and about the true being which is the object of that desire. With his erotics, Plato broke the ground for the development of an inquiry into desiring man that would lead in time to the Christian hermeneutics of the self. Foucault briefly studied the transition to the latter in the third volume of his history of sexuality, the formation of a culture of the self in the reflections of the moralists, philoso-phers and doctors in the first two centuries of our era.

This epoch sees major transitions in each of the Greek arts of self-conduct which Foucault examined. Roman dietetics operates within a context of increased medical concern with the body's pleasures, not just with respect to the possibility of their immoderate use but also in terms of their very nature. This tendency to pathologization emphasizes the particular danger that one's self could be carried passively by the de-mands of the body and the extravagance of desire in general. In economics, the relationships between men and women take on a greater reciprocity and new emphases are placed on one's duties to others. In erotics, there is a transfer to marriage of the traits which had been restricted to the friendship among males.[58] What is most significant for Foucault in the period of the Empire, however, is the context for these transitions: that culture's intensification of the self's interest in its relation to itself, and the establishment of the theme of "care of the self" at the center of moral preoccupation. The emergence of what Foucault calls the Roman "culture of the self" is rooted in the obligation its citizens felt themselves under to define new re-lations with the self. This obligation pressed on them for two principal reasons. First, the greater prevalence and signifi-cance of marriage as an institution required an elaboration of the self in the new context of affective relations between sexes. More important was a new problematization of political activ-ity. There was a need for the Roman citizen to clarify more fully his understanding of himself, for that self was challenged by an historically unparalled multiplicity of potential identities and conflicts created by imperial offices held, powers exercised and responsibilities shouldered.[59]

The care of the self which responded to this new sense of fragility of the individual was not just a vague concern but entailed an ensemble of diverse occupations and exercises directed to a more exact grasp of the self. The programs for the scrutiny of consciousness, methodical meditation on and written articulation of the self, developed in such groups as the Epicureans and Stoics, were aimed at the reinforcement of the rational self-control which promised a perfect government of the self and, thus, wise social conduct.[60] For Foucault, these practices, establishing a Roman government of the self, may be thought of as a sort of "permanent political relationship between self and self," or a "politics of themselves."[61] While the technology generated by a care of the self served the interests of self-mastery, it also testified to a new pleasure which the culture found in the very experience of the self. Concern with it was a "privilege-duty, a gift-obligation."[62] Despite the intensification of self-examination, however, Roman culture did not issue in a need for a hermeneutics of the self, because it did not fashion the self as an obscure text which required decipherment. Its interest was not in the discovery of the hidden and the unspoken, but rather with a constitution of the self according to a set of rational principles which are apprehended as rules for personal conduct. The techniques of self-examination and self-expression in this culture of the self aimed at a remembrance of principles which have been forgotten and which, through meditation, have the power to transform the self so as to make it a more efficient administrator of the self.[63] Nevertheless this form of care of the self was a transition from the unique relation of the self to truth in Greek experience to the later Christian hermeneutics of the self. This hermeneutics brought to a culmination the earliest development of that western man of desire whose reality was taken over by the modern period and forms the model for its quest of self-knowledge.

Freud's interpretation of **Oedipus** is an exemplification of that model of self-knowledge. Having solved the riddle of the Sphinx with the answer "man," Oedipus remains ignorant of his own identity. It is an ignorance which can be erased, however, for there exists a knowledge which will tell him who he is, once he assumes responsibility to seek his secret self, to become a subject to the truth by dependence upon a master of truth. The program for self-knowledge, embraced as a vehicle for discovering one's uniqueness, becomes a mere reenactment of the power-knowledge-subjectivity relations in modern culture. A quest for freedom gets diverted into a series of illusory liberations from repression. Although Foucault never presented the long history which led from antiquity and early Christianity to the modern subject, it is important to realize that, along with the modern age's appropriation of an earlier technology of the self, it also fundamentally changed the relation to the subject which that other age produced. Foucault's work already indicated the necessity for such a difference, because the earlier self is related to a sexual domain which cannot be identified with modern sexuality. The experience of love's pleasures or the self's desires, with both their dangers and illuminations, is radically distinct from the view of sexuality as a stubborn drive, forced to confront real or imaginary repressions. For Foucault, there were also two especially significant distortions for the subject. As opposed to both the Greek and Roman periods, the modern subject was fashioned in isolation from ethical and aesthetic concerns; truth itself becomes the uncontested ruler of human life. This tyranny of the scientific was strengthened by modernity's rejection of the cardinal element in Christian asceticism. Christian practices involved a renunciation of the self who was articulated. For the Christian, the truths of the self were always precarious, for they always related to the soul's continual conflict with the evil within itself. There could be no firm allegiance to a positive self, for there was no truth about the self which could not be utilized by the False One as a device for misleading and ensnaring the soul. Thus, the Christian always practiced a renunciation of the self who was articulated, a renunciation which mirrored, as I pointed out, the death to the self in baptism or martyrdom. The aim of modern knowledge and technologies of the self, however, is to foster the emergence of a positive self; one recognizes and attaches oneself to a self made available through the categories of psychological and psychoanalytic science and through the normative disciplines consistent with them. Thus, as was the case with Oedipus, we become victims of our own self-knowledge. For Foucault, this is an event of supreme political importance, because this victimization fashions the potentially transgressive dimension of the person into but another element of the disciplinary matrix which **Discipline and Punish** had described as the carceral archipelago. If the struggle with this modern power-knowledge-subjectivity formation is a politics of our selves, the key campaign in that struggle will be a new mode of fashioning an ethical way of being a self.

3. Ecstatic Thinking

Although it was only in his last writings that Foucault dealt explicitly with ethics, the ethical interest was decisive for his thought, from his first work thirty years earlier. In commenting on Binswanger's notion of the dream, Foucault claimed that dreams exhibit the essential meaning of human being to be a "radical liberty," the movement of existence which is the matrix within which self and world, subject and object make their appearance. Dream experience cannot be separated from its ethical content: "not because it may uncover secret inclinations, inadmissible desires, not because it may release the whole flock of instincts," but because it "restores the movement of freedom in its authentic meaning, showing how it establishes itself or alienates itself, how it constitutes itself as radical responsibility in the world, or how it forgets itself and abandons itself to its plunge into causality."[64] His evaluation of psychology as a human science was in terms of whether it achieved the proper goal of promoting the ill person's victory over the alienation which had made him a stranger to the reality of liberty, which he essentially is, and an outsider to the historical drama which is the stage for human fulfillment.[65] Foucault preserves his ethical interest through his other writings by restoring to the historical field what modernity had proclaimed as natural, and by approaching power and knowledge in terms not of what they are but rather what they do. In examining the force of knowledge-power relations, Foucault came to appreciate that the description of the human being as a radical liberty was incorrect because "man does not begin with liberty but with the limit."[66] He also appreciated that such a recognition need not lead to an abandonment of ethics itself, because the encounter with those limits created the opportunity for their transgression, for an ecstasy in both thought and action.

While Foucault's study of sexuality, and of Christianity in particular, opened up the domain of ethics for explicit consideration, there were two events in the political realm which motivated a concentration with ethics, events which were more significant for him than the election of a French Socialist government in 1981. The first was the Iranian Revolution of 1978–1979. His initially sympathetic viewpoint on it and its creators evoked sharp criticism in many French circles when the Shah's overthrow was followed by new executions and oppressions. In reply to this criticism, Foucault refused to dismiss the moral achievement of the Revolution when the political order inaugurated a new terror. He described his ethic as "anti-strategic," as irreducible to the question of political success: "In the end, there is no explanation for the man who revolts. His action is necessarily a tearing that breaks the thread of history and its long chains of reasons so that a man can genuinely give preference to the risk of death over the certitude of having james bernauer to obey."[67] This specific discrimination of the ethical was promoted by the emergence of the Solidarity movement in Poland, where Foucault had lived in 1958 and whose fortunes he followed closely in the years after. The suppression of the movement and the weak response of western governments to it encouraged him to recognize the political necessity for an ethics:

If we raise the question of Poland in strictly political terms, it is clear that we can quickly reach the point of saying that there's nothing we can do. We can't dispatch a team of paratroopers, and we can't send armored cars to liberate Warsaw. I think that, politically, we have to recognize this, but I think that we also agree that, for ethical reasons, we have to raise the problem of Poland in the form of a nonacceptance of what is happening there, and a nonacceptance of the passivity of our own governments. I think that this attitude is an ethical one, but it is also political; it does not consist in saying merely, "I protest," but in making of that attitude a political phenomenon that is as substantial as possible, and one which those who govern, here or there, will sooner or later be obliged to take into account.[68]

Foucault's own treatment of ethical life aimed to have a similar impact on those discourses which govern our approaches to good and evil.

The schema which he proposes for an analysis of ethical life mirrors the strangeness and effect of the passage from Borges on the Chinese definition of animals which opened **The Order of Things**: it wishes to shatter "all the familiar landmarks of my thought—our thought, the thought that bears the stamp of our age and our geography—breaking up all the ordered surfaces and all the planes with which we are accustomed to tame the wild profusion of existing things."[69] His model for an analysis of ethics in terms of the four distinct levels of ethical substance, mode of subjection, ethical work and telos was foreshadowed by Foucault's delineation of how the Christian pastorate transformed Hebraic themes of power.[70] It was provoked, however, by his realization that a history of moral codes or of the ways they were followed would not reach the more subtle level on which individuals fashion themselves as subjects of moral conduct and, thus, as desirous of a certain code and of conformity to it. On the level of codes, Western moralities betrayed an overwhelming similarity. The differences among them were disclosed by interrogating other levels of moral experience: What is regarded as the prime material of moral conduct (determination of ethical substance)? How does an individual establish his relation to a rule of conduct (mode of subjection)? What specific transformation of oneself is invited by an ethical commitment (ethical work)? At what mode of being does the ethical subject aim (*telos*)?[71] The posing of these questions to ancient and Christian experience uncovered a rich array of differences and modifications in each of the areas. The questions enabled Foucault himself to take a distance from how modernity problematized morality in terms of a subject of knowledge dependent on science.[72] He was able to turn to ethics as the field of a liberty forming itself as a subjectivization, that is, a "process in which the individual delimits that part of himself that will form the object of his moral practice, defines his position relative to the precept he will follow, and decides on a certain mode of being that will serve as his moral goal. And this requires him to act upon himself, to monitor, test, improve, and transform himself."[73]

The task of self-formation which Foucault puts forward has a specificity which reflects his own commitments as an intellectual. He is not seeking a form of morality generalizable for all, but rather developing a particular style which emerges from the history of his own freedom and thought.[74] Although his ethic extracts significant elements from both classical and Christian moralities, this recourse represents neither an idealization of nor a return to the premodern. The elements which he derives from earlier periods are integrated into a uniquely personal context, Foucault's effort to articulate himself as a moral thinker. In his last years, Foucault became more comfortable than he had been in the past with the profession of philosophy and he proposed that his entire work be approached in terms of its ambition to be a philosophical ethos, a philosophy-as-life, a way of acting in the contemporary world which manifests both a way of belonging to it as well as a task within it.[75] This ethos is exhibited most prominently in the philosopher's mode of thinking and one of the most striking features about Foucault's last period is the amount of attention which he gives to a meditation on thought itself.[76] I believe that these meditations were initially prompted by a harsh challenge to the worth of his efforts. Hadn't works such as **Discipline and Punish**, he was asked, created an anaesthetic effect on prison reformers, because his critique had an implacable logic which left no possible room for initiative? More generally, Is it really important to think, does criticism by intellectuals clear up anything?[77] Foucault's replies seek to redirect our expectations for thought away from either merely instrumental or grandly totalizing viewpoints on it. Thought should be subordinated neither to a government's social agenda, that "sacrilization of the social," which has often turned thinking into a function of administration, nor to that ambition which demands of it a "subversion of all codes" or "over-turning of all contemporary culture."[78] At the same time, he defends the achievements of his type of criticism: "I'll answer the claim that 'it did nothing.' There are hundreds and thousands of people who have worked toward the emergence of a certain number of problems, which today are actually being posed. To say that this did nothing is altogether wrong. Do you think that twenty years ago the problems of the relation between mental illness and psychological normality, the problem of the prison, the problem of medical power, the problem of the relations between the sexes, etc., . . . were being posed as they are posed today?"[79] Complementary to this defense is a new effort by Foucault to integrate his historical researches with the issue of the subject who must act, who is incited by that research to transform the real. This effort is reflected in his vision of thought as an essentially ethical activity: "Thought is freedom in relation to what one does, the motion by which one detaches oneself from it, establishes it as an object, and reflects on it as a problem."[80]

Foucault's ethic is the practice of an intellectual freedom which may be described as an ecstatic thinking or a worldly mysticism. Religious mystics had created a domain for an experience of revelation which was free of the need to follow the theologically sanctioned routes for encounter with supernatural reality. Foucault's work has opened a domain for the practice of a freedom which stands outside of the humanistic program for the conduct of human life and inquiry in history. Although it may seem strange to employ the model of mysticism for Foucault's thought, it is not an arbitrary imposition on my part. The severe techniques which he developed in his archaeological and genealogical methods of questioning, as ways of breaking the spell which humanism had placed on the modern mind, reintroduced into the contemporary landscape of thought that negative theology which had "prowled the borderlands of Christianity" for a millennium.[81]

Although Foucault never elaborated the analogy, negative theology was one of the few styles with which he explicitly compared his own thought.[82] His choice of the comparison is illuminating. It points first of all to Foucault's own experience of a fundamental personal conflict in his earlier intellectual interests as a "religious problem."[83] On the one hand, he was passionately involved in the new literary work of such writers as Georges Bataille and Maurice Blanchot, which displaced interest for him from a narrative of man to the being of the language within which images of the human are fashioned.[84] On the other hand, Foucault says he was attracted to the structuralist analysis carried out by the anthropologist, Claude

Levi-Strauss, and the historian of religion, Georges Dumézil, both of whom dispersed human reality among cultural structures. That Foucault considers the religious problem as the common denominator for both interests indicates that all four thinkers, although in very different ways, unleashed styles of reflection and forms of experience which overturned for him the accepted natural identity of man. Foucault's negative theology is a critique not of the conceptualizations employed for God but of that modern figure of finite man whose identity was put forward as capturing the essence of human being. Nevertheless, Foucault's critical thinking is best described as a negative theology, rather than a negative anthropology, for its flight from man is an escape from yet another conceptualization of the Absolute. The project of modernity was an absolutization of man, the passion to be, as Sartre saw, the "*Ens causa sui*, which religions call God."[85] Foucault explicitly recognized that Sartre's anthropology reflected a nineteenth century portrayal of man as an incarnated God.[86]

Foucault's negative theology is a subversion of that faith, an aim which permits us to appreciate its recourse to historical inquiry as a privileged mode of thought for him. Parallel to the death of God was an absolutization of man. Claiming a firm knowledge of this figure, humanism made humanity's happiness its ultimate goal and human perfection its permanent project. The place for humanism's actualization, however, was not the order of the supernatural but rather that of the historical. In history, purpose and progress could be found and man's victory and beatitude achieved. Uniting the development of modern thought and practice, the order of time became the Sacred History of Man. The religion of the God Humanity, with its priesthood of scientific experts as advanced in Comte's positivist philosophy, is not only an integral element of that philosophy but of the logic of the modern age itself.[87] Faced with a sacred history constituted by man's revelation to himself of his ever advancing perfection, Foucault has attempted to demythologize the historical reality in which the modern identity of man and the sources of his humanistic knowledges are lodged. That demythologization required more than an act of will; it demanded the ascetical methods for achieving a thought free of anthropology which Foucault developed, most especially in **The Archaeology of Knowledge**. In the light of his last works, it is clear that this asceticism served a greater liberation.

The negative theology which characterized the asceticism of Foucault's methods was a prelude to his conception of the philosophical life itself. He embraced Kant's definition of Enlightenment as an *Augsgang*, an exit or way out, because it corresponded to the central concern of his own work, the need to escape those prisons of thought and action which shape our politics, our ethics, our relations to our selves.[88] Embracing an ecstatic experiment beyond Kant, his last writings declare the need to escape our inherited relation to the self, a declaration which complements and intensifies his earlier announcement of the "death of man." "What can be the ethic of an intellectual—I accept the title of intellectual which seems at present to nauseate some people—if not that: to render oneself permanently capable of getting free of oneself." The motivation for his last works is identified as a special curiosity, the curiosity which "enables one to get free of oneself."[89] How is this desire to be understood? I believe that it must be approached on two levels. To appreciate either, one must dismiss the type of interpretation which asserts that Foucault's last works are a rehabilitation of the "Nietzschean distinction between the life-affirming character of pagan cultures over against the life-negating essence of the Judeo-Christian tradition." Within this perspective, Christian "self-renunciation" would be identified with "self-debasement."[90] Foucault saw more deeply. He recognized that, in addition to code-oriented moralities, Christianity developed ethics-oriented moralities, which were related to the "exercise of a personal liberty."[91] That liberty was paradoxical because it combined a care of the self with a sacrifice of the self: "Christian culture has developed the idea that if you want to take care of yourself in the right way you have to sacrifice yourself."[92] In Christianity, this sacrifice or mortification of the self reflected that dying to self in baptism and penance which we mentioned earlier. Foucault's desire to be free of the self presents a similar type of paradox.

On one level, it points back to his analysis of Christian hermeneutics. While he gave up its project of seeking a hidden self, he also appreciated the "great richness" of the ascetical moment of self-renunciation.[93] His regard for this self-denial was due to his understanding of how positive knowledge of the self often entails the obligation to identify oneself with the figure of that knowledge. He had long appreciated that the self could become a prison: "I am no doubt not the only one who writes in order to have no face."[94] On this level, Foucault's call for a renunciation of the self is basically the motto of a program for freedom as a thinker, a commitment to the task of permanent criticism. There is another more profound and interesting a level on which Foucault's desire should be understood. It derives from his personal experience, especially as it was shaped through his reading of Bataille and Blanchot. Both saw that Nietzsche's death of God did not provide the "mandate for a redefinition of man," but rather revealed a negativity without rest, which was created by the absence of absolute boundaries.[95] In his work, Bataille proclaimed that a morality after God's death was a morality which is "not centered on the guarantee of social and individual life given us by the 'main precepts' but on mystical passion leading man to die to himself in order to inherit eternal life. What it condemns is the dragging weight of attachment to the self, in the guise of pride and mediocrity and self-satisfaction."[96] In the epoch after man's death, there is a similar need for the mystical passion of an ecstatic transcendence of the self which seeks to put itself as a natural reality in the place of the Absent Absolute. Thought and life achieve ecstasy through a series of critiques which do not aim at an Absolute Emancipation but, rather, at experimental transgressions of the self. Foucault insisted on the necessity for developing new forms of relating to the self and he exhibited one. Perhaps it was most clearly expressed in the context of revolt: "It is through revolt that subjectivity (not that of great men but that of whomever) introduces itself into history and gives it the breath of life. A delinquent puts his life into the balance against absurd punishments; a madman can no longer accept confinement and the forfeiture of his rights; a people refuses the regime which oppresses it."[97] This breath of life or force of resistance, this Foucaultian spirituality, witnesses to the capacity for an ecstatic transcendence of any history which asserts its necessity. It also testifies to Foucault's subversion of any philosophical ideal of contemplative self-possession, and its replacement by a dispossession. The relation to the self is defined in terms of its worldly sources and its operations within the historical field. Such a relationship demands a task of stylization.

Despite Foucault's efforts to avoid such misinterpretations, his use of the notion of stylization, of an aesthetics of existence, has been taken as a sign of his allegiance to a Greek morality or to an a-moral aestheticism. Thus, he is accused of elevating the quest for beauty in life over all other intellectual and moral virtues with the result that the "**self** rather than the **world** and its inhabitants becomes the central focus of aesthetic enhancement." And so, it is claimed, "Foucault's standpoint favors either an attitude of narcissistic self-absorption or one of outwardly directed, aggressive self-aggrandizement."[98] Foucault's actual work achieves something very different. Rather than promoting a self-absorption, Foucault deprives the self of any illusion that it can become a sanctuary separated from the world. Just as his earlier work showed the radical dependence of the life of the mind on specific power-knowledge relations, so his last studies indicated how the classical moral experience of the self was shaped from medical, economic, and erotic problematizations. Foucault's notion of self-formation is always in the context of a struggle for freedom within an historical situation. It is why he refers to the subject as an "agonism," a "permanent provocation" to the knowledge, power and subjectivizations which operate on us.[99] This agonistic self is "not the decontextualized self of inwardness, but a self that becomes autonomous" only through a struggle with and a stylizing or adaptation of those concrete possibilities which present themselves as invitations for a practice of liberty.[100] Foucault's employment of aesthetic terms points to the power which this agonism has for an ecstatic art, for leaving itself behind in transgressing the prisons of a particular historical determination and for creating a new relation to event and, thus, self.

This ecstasy would be misunderstood if it was seen as a Nietzschean leap beyond common morality into an elitist superhuman status. In this interpretation, Foucault's work would terminate in a splendid solitude, foreign to any form of human solidarity and sense of common fate.[101] Foucault's practice of ethical and political solidarity in the cause of human rights is well-known.[102] This practice was carried through both in his life and in his theory. Unlike Nietzsche, Foucault identified with the weak and the vanquished, the mentally ill and the deviant, with the lives of such infamous people as Pierre Rivière and Herculine Barbin in whose accounts "one feels, under words polished like stone, the relentlessness and the ruin."[103] This identification motivated the movement of his thought toward an ever expanding embrace of otherness, an expansion that is the condition for any community of moral action. Rather than a replacement of intellectual and moral values, Foucault's aesthetics of existence wishes to place at the center of both thought and action the imaginative creativity which has been exiled to the exclusive practice of art. For him, the formation of oneself as a thinker and a moral agent, which develops only through historical struggles, must be understood as the creation of a work of art rather than the execution of a program. The energy of that work of art is an ecstasy, a transcendence of man and self which does not culminate in a Nietzschean Overman but in the recognition that, in leaving God and Man behind, we do not stand in need of a substitute for them.[104] Twenty years before his death, Foucault had tied the quest for liberty to research in the library: "Henceforth, the visionary experience arises from the black and white surface of printed signs, from the closed and dusty volume that opens with a flight of forgotten words." He claimed that the "fantastic is no longer a property of heart, nor is it found among the incongruities of nature; it evolves from the accuracy of knowledge, and its treasures lie dormant in documents."[105] Such a vision was equally distant from those who dreamed of a Total Enlightenment as it was from those who despaired of any sense. In an analogous way, his last writings acknowledge our impatience for liberty and our passion for ecstasy, but direct these not to the pursuit of some messianic age but to an engagement with the numberless potential transgressions of those forces which war against our self-creation and our solidarity.

Conclusion: Toward an Ethics of Thought.

It is far too early to predict what the ultimate legacy of Foucault's thought will be. Whatever weight his achievement carries for the future, we may be confident though that his thought will always be understood in the context of the historical period which evoked his particular anxiety and his unique voice. It was Foucault's fate to have lived at the end of that epoch which witnessed the catastrophic outcome of modern efforts to transform human beings according to a technology deduced from truth. Although his work investigated diverse issues, his project was a "history of truth," a challenging interrogation of that regime of truth under which we have lived and died for too long.[106] It was fitting, then, that the theme of Foucault's last courses and seminars was the practice of telling the truth (parrhesia) in ancient experience. His final research sought to indicate that the various forms of truth-telling which our culture has developed—philosophical, moral, scientific, political— were concrete responses to historical problematics. In his desire to problematize the truth-teller's role, Foucault's questions were: "Who is able to tell the truth? What are the moral, the ethical, and the spiritual conditions which entitle someone to present himself as, and to be considered as, a truth-teller? About what topics is it important to tell the truth? . . . What are the consequences of telling the truth? . . . What is the relation between the activity of truth-telling and the exercise of power?"[107] Although these questions will never become part of the larger, formal project which he envisioned for them, namely, a genealogy of the critical attitude in Western philosophy, they will remain as the echo of a long journey of thought. The impact of that thought on his readers is to make them acutely aware of their moral responsibility, as seekers or claimants of truth, to appreciate the sources and consequences of such searches and claims. Foucault exhibited in fresh ways how to doubt the order of things, and why such doubt must be practiced. He taught us to recognize that the articulation of a domain in terms of the true and the false is no less significant and dangerous in its implications than was the appearance of discourses which defined the holy and the profane, the saved and the damned, the good and the wicked. Looking from a more synoptic perspective than did his contemporaries, Foucault's future readers may well regard his diverse studies as elements in an ethical treatise for an intellectual practice that would be more self-critical. This treatise will be seen to respond to a loss of faith in the modern quest for enlightenment, to that new agnosticism which emerged from the tragedies of the twentieth century and from the dread of what current knowledge-power-subjectivity relations might yet make possible. Seen within this context, Foucault's schema for an analysis of ethics may be recognized as capturing both the major insights in his own thought's development as well as the distinct levels of his own treatise.

Foucault's 1963 examination of the novelist Raymond Roussel had been fascinated by Roussel's last gesture, the release of a posthumous volume in which he supposedly explained the techniques and aims of his obscure prose. In fact, Roussel's last work was far less the unveiling of a secret than it was the disclosure of the "underground force from which his language springs."[108] Foucault's final work imparts an analogous lesson. Foucault only came to the project and categories of that last stage by way of his previous efforts. The underground force which they disclose is a movement toward an ethics of thought. Foucault's distinct experiences of thought were not random experiments but join together to effect a common dynamism. The elements in his ethical schema had a long gestation period and mirror the four arts of interrogation which he practiced through his writings. (1) What was it necessary to think today in contrast to the traditional domain of the thought-worthy? What should the substance for thought be? (2) In examining this domain, what sort of understanding should be sought? What mode of subjection should the thinker take up? (3) How should the search for such understanding find its methodological way? What ascetical practices must it perform on itself in order to be enabled to think differently? (4) What goal is pursued through the definition of substance, mode of subjection, and practice of asceticism? Foucault's exploration of these questions throughout his works succeeded in creating a broad ethical inquiry on the activity of thought itself. It may be described as an ethical treatise, but it is not a general statement of a code for thinking nor even primarily an exemplary model for inquiry. Foucault's treatise, as it is encountered in his writings, constitutes a practice which educates his readers into an ethical responsibility for intellectual inquiry. It provides not an obligatory conduct but a possible escape from an intellectual milieu unnourished by ethical interrogation. Foucault's practice of his ethic marks paths for a collaborative assumption of new responsibilities.

The ethical substance of his treatise puts forward a domain for analysis which overcomes the theory-practice dualism. It is composed, not of institutions, theories or ideologies but of practices, the discursive and extra-discursive relations which are operative in a culture's program for the conduct of intellectual pursuit, of practical action, and of self-constitution. Foucault's ethical perspective was signaled in his concern with the action of the axes: what knowledge does (and not reads), how power constructs (and not represents), how a relationship to the self is invented (and not discovered). Philosophical inquiry becomes substantially ethical, in a Foucaultian sense, when it is concerned with the problematizations which pose themselves to a culture as a result of the interplay of its practices: its types of knowledge, its political strategies, and its styles of personal life. The focus for an analysis of the ethical substance is the thought which responds to these problematizations or which inhabits these practices, if thought is understood as the "way people begin to take care of something, of the way they become anxious about this or that— for example, about madness, about crime, about sex, about themselves, or about truth."[109] The mode of subjection suggested by Foucault's treatise is a commitment to a history of the present, an examination of experience in terms of, though not restricted to, three major axes: an axis of knowledge (where a discourse directing comprehension is formed), an axis of power (where a normativity is produced), and an axis of ethics (where a particular relation of the self to the self is constituted). The effect of such a history is to exhibit present practices not as the necessary outcome of an evolutionary process but as a field of contingencies, to which our future is not held hostage. Such inquiry into the present is "indissociable from a desperate eagerness to imagine it, to imagine it otherwise than it is, and to transform it not by destroying it but by grasping it in what it is."[110] The asceticism of his treatise is contained in the exacting arts of questioning which he developed in the archaeological-genealogical methods for analyses of discursive formations, power-knowledge deployments, and ethical systems. All these methods are in the service of a strategic negative theology, which subverts the status of Absolute Man as the unworldly creator of his knowledge, politics and ethics.

The discrimination of each of these levels is indebted to Foucault's earlier experiences of thought and their transformation of Kant's questions regarding human knowledge, obligation and aspiration into historical investigations. The result is that james bernauer philosophy as anthropology is overcome by an ecstatic thinking which transgresses the universal, necessary and obligatory. Foucault realized that there was never to be a definitive escape from configurations of knowledge-power-self relations and yet he was unyielding in his conviction that no specific configuration was necessary and unchangeable. His ecstatic thinking counseled escape from those relationships to self which we have inherited as children of western technologies for thought and for self-development. For Foucault, there was a special pleasure to be discovered in thinking, in transgressing the limits laid down by intellectual disciplines and in meeting once again the mystery of a history that needed to be newly recognized as thoughtworthy and as open to artistic transformation. If, as a result, his philosophy is described as an "anarchism," it is only because the modern bureaucratization of intellectual life has made it so difficult to practice the freedom and experience the pleasure of thinking.[111] Such is the goal of Foucault's treatise.

Whatever conclusions his future readers may draw, Foucault's thought made it more difficult for his contemporaries to think unhistorically, non-politically, a-ethically, that is, irresponsibly.[112] Perhaps, as has recently been charged, his thought is "not a shout of joy."[113] But, it should be asked, when did that become the standard for evaluating a thinker? As far as Foucault's work is concerned, we will have to be satisfied with hearing a voice which suffered with some of the victims not only of obvious captivities but also of modern liberties and their programs. As a result, it was a thought which struggled impatiently for new practices of freedom. Ultimately, it was a cry of spirit.

Boston College

NOTES

1. Michel Foucault, **Mental Illness and Psychology**, trans. by Alan Sheridan (New York: Harper Colophon, 1976), p. 87.

2. On his earliest anthropological project, see Foucault's **Maladie mentale et personnalité** (Paris: Presses Universitaires de France, 1954) and his introduction to Ludwig Binswanger's **Le rêve et l'existence** (Paris: Desclée De Brouwer, 1954), pp. 9–128. The latter work has been translated by Forrest Williams as "Dream, Imagination and Existence," in the **Review of Existential Psychology and Psychiatry** XIX, 1 (1984–85), pp. 29–78.

3. **The Order of Things: An Archaeology of the Human Sciences** (New York: Pantheon, 1971), p. xxiv.

4. The major works in this period are Foucault's 1969 **The Archaeology of Knowledge**, trans. A.M. Sheridan Smith (New York: Harper Colophon, 1976) and his 1970 inaugural lecture at the Collège de France which is published as an appendix to the **Archaeology**, "The Discourse on Language," pp. 215–237. My characterization of this form of thinking as dis-

sonant reflects Foucault's debt to the world of music. He tells us that he was first ripped from the dialectical universe in which he had been living by the experience of music, by listening to those contemporary French representatives of serial and twelve-tone music Barraqué and Boulez. (Cf. the 1967 Italian interview conducted by P. Caruso and published in his **Conversazione con Levi-Strauss, Foucault, Lacan** [Milano: U. Musia and Co., 1969], p. 117.) Schoenberg defines the character of such music as the "emancipation of dissonance." Cf. Foucault's later discussion with Boulez, "La musique contemporaine et le public," **FNAC Magazine** 15 (1983), pp. 10–12. For two recent reflections on Foucault's relation to music, see "Quelques souvenirs de Pierre Boulez," an interview with Alain Jaubert in **Critique** 471–472 (August-September, 1986), pp. 745–747, and Michel Fano, "Autour de la musique," **Le débat** 41 (Sept.–Nov., 1986), pp. 137–139.

5. "The Discourse on Language," p. 231.

6. The major texts of this period are the 1975 **Discipline and Punish: The Birth of the Prison**, trans. Alan Sheridan (New York: Pantheon, 1977) and the 1976 **The History of Sexuality I: An Introduction**, trans. by Robert Hurley (New York: Pantheon Books, 1978).

7. Daraki, "Michel Foucault's Journey to Greece," **Telos** 67 (Spring, 1986), p. 105; Wolin, "Foucault's Aesthetic Decisionism" in the same issue of **Telos**, p. 78.

8. For my remarks on Foucault's 1975 course I am indebted to a transcription of several of the lectures as well as the course description published in **Annuaire du Collège de France** 75 (1975), pp. 335–339; in a March 1980 conversation, Foucault told me of Illich's suggestion to him; "The Discourse on Language," p. 232.

9. **The History of Sexuality I**, p. 61.

10. Course lecture of February 19, 1975.

11. For example, in his 1983 discussion, "On the Genealogy of Ethics: An Overview of Work in Progress" in Hubert Dreyfus and Paul Rabinow, **Michel Foucault: Beyond Structuralism and Hermeneutics**, 2nd edition (Chicago: University of Chicago Press, 1983), pp. 229–264, and in his account of his project's modifications in the second volume of his history of sexuality, **The Use of Pleasure**, trans. by Robert Hurley (New York: Pantheon, 1985), pp. 3–13.

12. **The History of Sexuality I**, p. 143.

13. **Ibid.**, p. 146.

14. The titles are listed on the back cover of the original French edition of the first volume. Also, see **The History of Sexuality I**, pp. 21, 104–105, 113–114.

15. Cf. his course descriptions of these years, which appeared in English as "War in the Filigree of Peace" (1976), trans. by Ian Mcleod, **The Oxford Literary Review** 4:2 (1980), pp. 15–19; "Foucault at the Collège de France" I & II (1978, 1979), trans. by James Bernauer, **Philosophy and Social Criticism** 8:2–3 (Summer and Fall, 1981), pp. 235–242, 351–359.

16. Foucault, "Governmentality," **I & C** 6 (Autumn, 1979), p. 6. This is a translation of an important lecture from Foucault's 1978 course.

james bernauer

17. Foucault's summary of the 1980 course may be found in the **Annuaire du Collège de France** 80 (1980), pp. 449–452. The Stanford lectures were published as "Omnes et Singulatim: Towards a Criticism of 'Political Reason,'" in **The Tanner Lectures on Human Values** II, edited by R. Aron et al. (Salt Lake City: University of Utah Press, 1981), pp. 225–254. Other publications are: "Sexuality and Solitude," **Humanities in Review** I (1982), edited by David Rieff (New York: Cambridge University Press, 1982), pp. 3–21; "The Battle for Chastity," in **Western Sexuality: Practice and Precept in Past and Present Times**, edited by Philippe Ariès and André Béjin (Oxford: Basil Blackwell, 1985), pp. 14–25; "L'écriture de soi," **Corps écrit** 5 (1983), pp. 3–23. In addition, there are several discussions: "On the Genealogy of Ethics" in **Michel Foucault: Beyond Structuralism and Hermeneutics**; "The Regard for Truth," **Art and Text** 16 (Summer, 1984), pp. 20–31; and "Final Interview" **Raritan** V,1 (Summer, 1985), pp. 1–13. There are also several observations in **The Use of Pleasure** as well as **The Care of the Self**, trans. by Robert Hurley (New York: Pantheon, 1986). A closely related summer course, "The Discourse of Self-Disclosure," was presented at the University of Toronto in 1982. In November, 1980, he presented two important lectures at Dartmouth College: "Subjectivity and Truth" and "Christianity and Confession." I was able to attend the 1980 and 1982 courses and have transcripts of the Dartmouth lectures.

18. "Omnes et Singulatim: Towards a Criticism of 'Political Reason,'" pp. 228–231, 236–238.

19. **Ibid.**, p. 237. Lectures from the 1980 course on March 19th and 26th.

20. "Sexuality and Solitude," p. 14.

21. **Ibid.**, pp. 10–11.

22. 1980 course, lectures of March 5 and 12; "Christianity and Confession"; Toronto course, "The Discourse of Self-Disclosure," June 15, 1982.

23. "The Battle for Chastity," p. 25; 1980 course, lecture of March 26th.

24. "The Battle for Chastity," p. 25. For a study of the important fifth-century leader of monasticism, Cassian, cf. Owen Chadwick's **John Cassian** (Cambridge: Cambridge University Press, 1968).

25. **Ibid.**, p. 23. "Christianity and Confession"; "Sexuality and Solitude," pp. 15–16; Toronto course, "The Discourse of Self-Disclosure," June 15, 1982.

26. "Christianity and Confession."

27. "Sexuality and Solitude," p. 10.

28. "Foucault's summary for his 1982 course in **Annuaire du Collège de France**" (82), p. 403.

29. "The Battle for Chastity," p. 25.

30. Cf. "Omnes et Singulatim: Towards a Criticism of 'Political Reason,'" p. 239; "Christianity and Confession"; Toronto course, "The Discourse of Self-Disclosure," June 15, 1982; "Sexuality and Solitude," pp. 10, 15; **The Use of Pleasure**, pp. 63, 70.

31. **Herculine Barbin dite Alexina B.** (Paris: Gallimard, 1978). Foucault's essay was published as the introduction to the English translation of the

work, **Herculine Barbin, Being the Recently Discovered Memoirs of a Nineteenth Century Hermaphrodite**, trans. by Richard McDougall (New York: Pantheon, 1980), pp. vii-xvii.

32. **Herculine Barbin, Being . . .** , p. 144.

33. "Omnes et Singulatim: Towards a Criticism of 'Political Reason,' " p. 239.

34. Foucault, "The Subject and Power," in Dreyfus and Rabinow, **Beyond Structuralism and Hermeneutics**, p. 215.

35. "Sexuality and Solitude," pp. 11, 16.

36. "Christianity and Confession."

37. "The Subject and Power," pp. 212, 216.

38. **The Use of Pleasure**, p. 251.

39. "Politics and Ethics: An Interview" (1983) in **The Foucault Reader**, edited by Paul Rabinow (New York: Pantheon, 1984), p. 375.

40. **The Use of Pleasure**, p. 5.

41. "What Is Enlightenment?," in **The Foucault Reader**, p. 46.

42. **The History of Sexuality** I, p. 130. I treat this archaeology within the perspective of psychosis in a forthcoming essay, "Oedipus, Freud, Foucault: Fragments of an Archaeology of Psychoanalysis," to be published in the collection edited by David M. Levin, **Pathologies of the Modern Self: Challenges to the Orthodoxy** (New York: New York University Press, 1987).

43. **Madness and Civilization**, trans. by Richard Howard (New York: Mentor, 1967), p. 162; **The Order of Things**, p. 361; cf. Foucault's **Mental Illness and Psychology**, p. 87.

44. **The History of Sexuality** I, p. 119.

45. S. Freud, **The Interpretation of Dreams** in **The Standard Edition** IV, edited by James Strachey (London: Hogarth, 1973), p. 262.

46. "Introduction to Pfister's **The Psycho-Analytic Method**" (1913) in **The Standard Edition** XII, edited by James Strachey (London: Hogarth, 1973), p. 329.

47. **The Birth of the Clinic**, pp. 153, 198.

48. Cf. **Madness and Civilization**, pp. 216–222, and **The Birth of the Clinic**, p. 199.

49. **The Order of Things**, p. 361.

50. "Introduction" to **Herculine Barbin**, p. xi. Cf. **The History of Sexuality** I, pp. 104–105, 68, 70.

51. **The History of Sexuality** I, pp. 82–83; cf. pp. 103–114, 130.

52. Cf. **The Use of Pleasure**, Parts II, "Dietetics," and III, "Economics," pp. 95–184.

53. **The Use of Pleasure**, pp. 221–225.

54. **Ibid.**, p. 221.

55. **Ibid.**, pp. 220–221.

56. **Ibid.**, p. 88.

57. **Ibid.**, p. 240.

58. Cf. **The Care of the Self**, parts IV, "The Body," V, "The Wife," and VI, "Boys," pp. 97–232.

59. Cf. **The Care of the Self**, part III, "Self and Others," pp. 69–95.

60. Cf. **The Care of the Self**, part II, "The Cultivation of the Self," pp. 37–68.

61. "On the Genealogy of Ethics," p. 246.

62. **The Care of the Self**, p. 47.

63. Cf. Foucault's 1982 course description, "Histoire des systèmes de pensée," **Annuaire du Collège de France** (1982), pp. 395–406; "L'écriture de soi," pp. 3–23.

64. "Dream, Imagination, and Existence," pp. 51,52.

65. **Maladie mentale et personnalité**, pp. 109–110; cf. "Dream, Imagination, and Existence," pp. 74–75.

66. "La folie, l'absence d'oeuvre," (1964), published as appendix to the 1972 edition of **Histoire de la folie** (Paris: Gallimard), p. 578.

67. Foucault, "Is it useless to revolt?"(1979), trans. by James Bernauer, **Philosophy and Social Criticism** 8 (Spring, 1981), p. 5.

68. "Politics and Ethics: An Interview," p. 377. For Foucault's viewpoint on Poland and the crisis generated by Solidarity, cf. "En abandonnant les Polonais, nous renonçons à une part de nous-mêmes," **Le Nouvel Observateur** 935 (Oct. 9, 1982), p. 36; "L'expérience morale et sociale des Polonais ne peut plus être effacée," **Les nouvelles littéraires** 2857 (Oct. 14–20, 1982), pp. 8–9; "La Pologne, et après? Edmond Maire: Entretiens avec Michel Foucault," **Le débat** 25 (May, 1983), pp. 3–34. For a personal recollection of Foucault in Poland, see the essay by the former French Ambassador, Étienne Burin des Roziers, "Une rencontre à Varsovie," **Le débat** 41 (Sept.-Nov., 1986), pp. 132–136.

69. **The Order of Things**, p. xv.

70. Cf. "Omnes et Singulatim: Towards a Criticism of 'Political Reason,'" pp. 236–239.

71. **The Use of Pleasure**, pp. 26–28.

72. Cf. "On the Genealogy of Ethics," pp. 236, 251–252.

73. **The Use of Pleasure**, p. 28.

74. "Final Interview," trans. by T. Levin and I. Lorenz, **Raritan** V,1 (Summer, 1985), p. 12.

75. Cf. **Ibid.**, p. 2; "What Is Enlightenment?," p. 39; and "Politics and Ethics: An Interview," p. 375.

76. For example, cf. the first preface he wrote for the second volume of the history of sexuality in **The Foucault Reader**, pp. 336–338; "Polemics,

Politics and Problematizations," an interview conducted by Paul Rabinow in **The Foucault Reader**, pp. 388–389.

77. Foucault, "Questions of Method," trans. by Colin Gordon, **Ideology and Consciousness** 8 (Spring, 1981), p. 11; "Is it really important to think?," trans. by T. Keenan, **Philosophy and Social Criticism** 9,1 (Spring, 1982), p. 33.

78. "Is it really important to think?," p. 33; "Questions of Method," p. 11.

79. "Is it really important to think?," p. 33.

80. "Polemics, Politics, and Problematizations," p. 388. As examples of his desire to claim coherence, cf. **The Use of Pleasure**, pp. 11–12; "Final Interview," and the opening pages of the interview published in this issue, "The Ethics of Care of the Self as the Practice of Freedom," trans. by Joseph Gauthier.

81. "La pensée du dehors," **Critique** 229 (June, 1966), p. 526. I elaborate this theme of negative theology as the central experience of Foucault's thought in a forthcoming article, "The Prisons of Man: An Introduction to Foucault's Negative Theology," to be published in the **International Philosophical Quarterly** (December, 1987).

82. "La pensée du dehors," pp. 526–527. The analogy was employed again in a lecture at the Collège de France on January 30, 1980.

83. In a 1967 interview with P. Caruso published in Caruso's **Conversazione con Levi-Strauss, Foucault, Lacan** (Milano: U. Musia and Co., 1969), p. 120. In the context of this religious interest, it is interesting to note that in 1957, while he was in Sweden, Foucault offered a course devoted to "religious experience in French literature from Chateaubriand to Bernanos." (Cf. Jean Piel, "Foucault à Uppsala," **Critique** 471–2 [Aug.-Sept., 1986], p. 749.)

84. Bataille's dialogue with negative theology runs throughout his writings. Cf. Roger Verneaux, "L'athéologie mystique de Georges Bataille," **Recherches de philosophie** III-IV: **De la connaissance de Dieu** (1958), pp. 125–158.

85. Jean-Paul Sartre, **Being and Nothingness** (New York: Washington Square Press, 1966), p. 784.

86. Cf. "Foucault répond à Sartre," **La Quinzaine Littéraire** 46 (March 1–15, 1968), pp. 20–22. However Foucault's faith or absence of it be described, it seems singularly inappropriate to claim, as Jean-Marie Auzias has in his recent book, that "radical atheism" is the point of convergence between Sartre and Foucault. On this topic, too, the two thinkers would be quite far from one another. (Cf. Auzias, **Michel Foucault** [Paris: La Manufacture, 1986], p. 240.)

87. Cf. Eric Voegelin's collection of essays edited by John Hallowell, **From Enlightenment to Revolution** (Durham, N.C: Duke University Press, 1975), especially "The Apocalypse of Man: Comte," pp. 136–159.

88. Cf. "What Is Enlightenment?," p. 34.

89. "The Regard for Truth," p. 29; **The Use of Pleasure**, p. 8.

90. Wolin, "Foucault's Aesthetic Decisionism," p. 83.

james bernauer

91. "Une esthétique de l'existence," a conversation between MF and Alessandro Fontana in **Le Monde** (July 15–16, 1984), p. xi. Cf. **The Use of Pleasure**, p. 30.

92. "The Power and Politics of Michel Foucault," an interview with MF in the **Daily Californian** (April 22, 1983), p. 20.

93. "Christianity and Confession."

94. **The Archaeology of Knowledge,** p. 17.

95. Allan Stoekl, **Politics, Writing, Mutilation** (Minneapolis: University of Minnesota Press, 1985), p. 109.

96. Georges Bataille, **Death and Sensuality** (New York: Walker and Company, 1962), pp. 229–230.

97. "Is it useless to revolt?," p. 8.

98. Wolin, "Foucault's Aesthetic Decisionism," pp. 84,85.

99. "The Subject and Power," p. 222.

100. Reiner Schürmann, "What Can I Do? in an Archaeological- Genealogical History," **The Journal of Philosophy** 82, #10 (October, 1985), p. 545.

101. For examples of this view, see Stephen White, "Foucault's Challenge to Critical Theory" **American Political Science Review** 80, #21 (June, 1986), pp. 428–430; Daraki, *op. cit.*, p. 108.

102. For accounts of Foucault's political work, cf. Claude Mauriac's **Le temps immobile** 3: **Et comme l'espérance est violente** (Paris: Grasset, 1976), especially pp. 261–592; and Bernard Kouchmer, "Un vrai samourai," in **Michel Foucault: Une histoire de la vérité** (Paris: Syros, 1985), pp. 85–89.

103. "The Life of Infamous Men,"(1977) in Michel Foucault, **Power, Truth, Strategy**, edited by Meaghan Morris and Paul Patton (Sydney: Feral, 1979), p. 77.

104. I believe that Gilles Deleuze's sensitive study, **Foucault** (Paris: Editions de Minuit, 1986) errs in linking Foucault too closely with Nietzschean aspirations. Foucault has transcended even them.

105. Foucault, "Fantasia of the Library," in **Language, Counter- Memory, Practice**, p. 90.

106. **The Use of Pleasure**, p. 11; cf. **The History of Sexuality** I, p. 60.

107. "Discourse and Truth," p. 113.

108. **Death and the Labyrinth: The World of Raymond Roussel**, trans. by Charles Ruas (Garden City, N.Y.: Doubleday and Company, 1986), p. 7.

109. "Discourse and Truth," p. 48; cf. "Polemics, Politics and Problematizations," p. 390; on Foucault's notion of practices, cf. his "Questions of Method," pp. 3–14.

110. "What Is Enlightenment?," p. 41.

81

111. On Foucault as an anarchist, cf. Reiner Schürmann, "What Can I Do? in an Archaeological-Genealogical History." On the problem of the bureau-

cratization of intellectual life, there is, of course, an enormous literature. Recent studies which have discussed the problem are Paul Bové, **Intellectuals in Power: A Genealogy of Critical Humanism** (New York: Columbia University Press, 1986), and **The Authority of Experts: Studies in History and Theory**, edited by Thomas L. Haskell (Bloomington: Indiana University Press, 1984).

112. Space does not allow me to develop the argument that it is precisely Foucault's ethic of thought which accounts for his work's appeal among his major commentators. Their disagreements with one another have often obscured the very dissimilar levels on which they are reading him. This difference of levels has occulted how the major criticial perspectives on his work have been shaped by a critic's affinity to one of the elements in Foucault's ethic with the others relegated to the shadows. The fact that these readings mirror his own ethical strategies perhaps witnesses to a widespread yearning for such an ethic of thought. This schema for the interpretation of commentary on Foucault may only be suggested here. **Ethical substance**: its *knowledge* axis is the interest of the Nietzschean treatments of Alan Sheridan (**Michel Foucault: The Will to Truth** [New York: Tavistock-Methuen, 1980]) and Deleuze (**Foucault**); the *power* axis is the focus of the Marxist perspectives of Mark Poster (**Foucault, Marxism and History: Mode of Production versus Mode of Information** [New York: Blackwell, Polity Press, 1984]) and Barry Smart (**Foucault, Marxism and Critique** [Boston: Routledge and Kegan Paul, 1983]); on the *subject* axis, it is Foucault's excavation of liberalism and that system's production of the personal which interests Jeffrey Minson (**Genealogies of Morals: Nietzsche, Foucault, Donzelot and the Eccentricity of Ethics** [New York: St. Martin's Press, 1985]). The **mode of subjection** attracts other critics: Mark Cousins and Athar Hussain (**Michel Foucault** [New York: St. Martin's Press, 1984]), Hubert Dreyfus and Paul Rabinow (**Michel Foucault: Beyond Structuralism and Hermeneutics**). It is the **asceticism** of Foucault's work which provides the level for the interpretations of Karlis Racevskis (**Michel Foucault and the Subversion of Intellect** [Ithaca, N.Y.: Cornell University Press, 1983]), Pamela Major-Poetzl (**Michel Foucault's Archaeology of Western Culture: Toward a New Science of History** [Chapel Hill: University of North Carolina Press, 1983]), Charles Lemert and Garth Gillan (**Michel Foucault: Social Theory as Transgression** [New York: Columbia University Press, 1982]). The **goal** of Foucault's ethic is the concern of John Rajchman (**Michel Foucault: The Freedom of Thought** [New York: Columbia University Press, 1985]).

113. Daraki, ''Michel Foucault's Journey to Greece,'' p. 110.

82

diane rubenstein

food for thought: metonymy in the late foucault

We serve no babies.
(Sign in Sen Yon Chinese restaurant, Lafayette, Indiana)

Once this lady called me up and said, "Are you a gay restaurant?" And I said, "No, we serve seafood."[1]
(Marvin Paige, owner of Claire's restaurant)

I. Two purveyors of gustatory pleasure reveal a predilection for metonymy in the service of a politics of exclusion. Their semiotic strategies vary somewhat: Harry Liu places a written sign at the entrance to his Chinese restaurant. Marvin Paige, eager to avoid an onslaught of yuppie patrons after a favorable **New York Times** review strategically places a few transvestites at the bar. In many ways these two restauranteurs represent two limit cases of metonymy and discursive self-awareness. Harry Liu is blind to any possible Swiftian reading of his sign—the metonymy "no babies" simply signifies a resistance to family dining. (Or, perhaps, given the homogenizing tendencies of midwest cuisine which efface all ethnic differences, the resistance to family dining is only a secondary signifier to further differentiate his restaurant from Denny's next door.) Liu's metonymy "no babies" can be subsumed into the canon of standard metonymy: crown for monarch, sail for ship as in Genette's terminology, a metonymy of content (*metonymie de contenant*).[2] Or, it can be seen in relation to the definition of Mauss. Metonymy can be recorded as the relation of contiguity of the part to the remainder.[3] If babies can be read as a contracted form of families with babies, Paige's subversive metonymy "gay restaurant" signifies that this is really a **neighborhood** place:[4] "I wanted to keep Claire a neighborhood place. It's not just gay—they're people who understand everyone's lifestyle." Both Paige and Liu choose metonymy to subvert or resist metonymic contagion, or to differentiate their establishments from a perceived enviromental threat: for Liu, the prevalence of family-style restaurants (Bob Evans, Denny's, Waffle House) located on the same signifying chain/strip; for Paige, to avoid contamination of his neighborhood clientele by atopic yuppies. Consideration of place is important in both cases. (The location of Paige's Claire in Chelsea is a definite *atout*.) And, after all, metonymy is the figure *par excellence* of place. Indeed, commentators have bemoaned the reduction of metonymy to spatial considerations—contiguity—which resulted from Jakobson's bipolar schema.[5]

Yet if both Paige and Liu use metonymy to subvert or resist another form of metonymic contagion, Paige's play on "gay restaurant . . . serve seafood" is more deliberate and one might add, perversely metonymic. It is Paige who thus most resembles the strict Lacanian in his choice of transvestite as barrier. For Lacan, metonymy most differed from metaphor in the impossibility of the signified from ever crossing the bar.[6] The choice of transvestites—a particular form of exchange of sexual signifiers which doesn't cross the bar of sexuality, unlike transexuals—forms a delicious *en abime*. **Transvestites as barrier to prevent prospective yuppie patrons from crossing the *bar*.** Homonymia at the service of homophobia.

And we might be bold enough to take our restaurant metonymies to their appropriate Lacanian conclusion: the role of metonymy as *Verschiebung* (displacement).[7] In psychoanalytic theory, this is the main method by which the unconscious gets around censorship (and the yuppie gets by headwaiters) as it also indicates "the place of the subject in the search for the truth" (or dinner . . .).[8]

II. *What we have to do with banal facts is to discover—or try to discover—which specific and perhaps original problem is connected with them.*[9]
Michel Foucault

But how does our excursus via restaurant metonyms inform our understanding of Foucault's most recent volumes? Why begin a communication on Foucault with such a gratuitous explication? One could cite Foucault's penchant for writing the history of the seemingly trivial, marginal or, at least, eccentric. No subject is beneath contempt; even yuppies are entitled to a post-structuralist designer genealogy.

One might also cite the uncanny similarity between Foucault's interviews with Dreyfus and Rabinow: "Sex is boring . . . (the Greeks) were not much interested in sex, it was not a great issue. Compare for instance, what they had to say about the place of food and diet." Indeed, some of the most compelling and lyrical sections of **Usage de Plaisirs** and **Le Souci de Soi** are those that concern diet and body.[10] The privileging of food over sex, prevalent in Greece and in the early Christian era ("The problem was food, food, food . . .") is echoed by a recent **NY Post** poll: "If given the choice between having dinner at one of the best restaurants in New York or having sex, you'd choose dining out, you are not alone. 61% of women polled and 40% of men opted for a good meal."[11] If the diet forms a crucial part of Foucault's self-forming practices, Yuppie self-definition is above all "Where, how and what they eat."[12]

But shouldn't one be wary of any analogies between Greeks and Yuppies? If Foucault has said in another context that another era cannot be exemplary for us,[13] is there any valid association between Yuppies and Foucault's Greeks, apart from the obvious literalization of Greek as fraternity comportment: "You get a lot of groups. It's a post-college fraternity phenomenon. When they're in groups they always act out."[14] Is Yuppie Greek comportment then to be read as an inversion of the *hubris* extolled by Foucault's subjects? A mirror form of the austere and beautiful life so limpidly evoked by Foucault? Or do they serve as a counter example? For if modern society is characterized by the constitution of a "deep self" with a true sexuality, Yuppies represent the Lacanian chain of dead desire.[15]

I prefer to evoke Yuppies with a certain poignancy for metonymy in the search for truth or truth effects. Moreover, it is this pathetic attempt to constitute a self in the absence of any principle of identity that most clearly distinguishes the Yuppie from those enlightened denizens of Berkeley (invoked by Foucault) who appear to be in touch with Foucault's *technè tou biou* (practices of the self which make the life a work of art).[16] Foucault is aware of the possible misreading of his two volumes as the penultimate self-help book. (Indeed, the initial critcal reception in France heralded **Usage** as "the beach book of the summer."[17]) Yet the Berkeley enthusiasts of the self who ". . . think everything that they do from the way they eat breakfast to the way they have sex . . . should be perfected" mistakenly believe that they know the truth about desire, life, nature, and the body.

The Yuppie, in contrast, resembles those patients of Roman Jakobson with selection deficiency.[18] In other words, they are unable to imitate; they can only appropriate.[19] "They have all the instincts of a chameleon with none of its ability."[20] Contagion and contiguity are essential: "They **jump on** an idea, an artist, a restaurant, a neighborhood . . ." Proximity substitutes for judgment:[21]

*They deify certain artists: Philip Glass, Wyndham Hill music.
Word gets out it's ok to listen to them . . . Julian Schnabel . . .
They went in droves to Caravaggio, Van Gogh, Picasso. That
was easy.* **Deciding where to go for brunch was the hard
part.**

Similarity disorder/selection deficiency brings us to the second
feature of metonymy illustrated by Yuppies' purported behavior. Impaired selection, presupposition by contiguity never leads
to hermeneutical understanding. Rather the logic of appropriation over imitation displaces importance away from the
true to its effect. In other words, it is the *vraisemblable* (rea-
sonable, likely, probable) and not the *vrai* (true) that is the
object of the Yup's quest: "They assume they take on all the
qualities of the object and more often than not they are
wrong."[22] The importance of this substitution of truth effect/
vraisemblance for the true (*vrai*) for a theory of metonymy has
been noted by Todorov and Barthes.[23] Todorov sees the de-
tective-novel genre as a tension between *vraisemblance/ver-
ité*. Or the genre depends on the assumption that what is likely
isn't true.[24] Barthes' seminal "Real Effect" situates the truth
of characters' psyches displayed metonymically through a series of descriptive details: Anna Karenina's "handbag," Flaubert's "barometer," Michelet's "little door." It is this real effect
that is at the foundation of literary modernism. We could also
cite the more appropriate Foucaultian example of the play
between cell and corridor, public and private spaces inscribed
in an architecture of tenements that forms the text of Zola's
L'Assomoir. However, unlike the initial metonyms of Cubist
paintings, Yuppie truth effects are never transformed into a
set of meaningful synecdoches.[25] Indeed, the distinction of
Foucault's metonyms presented in **Usage** is that they are
recuperated in a synecdochal schema in **Souci de Soi**. Yet
these differences between metonymy and synecdoche may
be more apparent than real, depending ultimately upon one's
own discursive strategy. Genette writes: "We thus see that
at the limit all metonymy is convertible to synecdoche by appealing to the higher ensemble, and all synecdoche into metonymy through recourse to the relation between the constituent parts."[26] We will be focusing on the reduction of
synecdochal schema into the metonyms (of aphrodesia) discussed among the constituent parts of **Usage de Plaisirs**.

Todorov warns of the dangers of the *vraisemblable* and the
impossibility of discussing truth and tropes. If metonymy and
synecdoche are locked into a perspectival dance, the *vraisemblable* forbids us evading its clutches and also from talking
about it.

*The vraisemblable tracks us everywhere and we can not
escape him. The constitutive law of our discourse constrains
us from it. If I speak, my enunciation would obey a certain law
and inscribe itself in a vraisemblance that I can not make
explicit and reject without making use of another enunciation
whose law would be implicit. Through the skew of the enunciation, my discourse will always give rise to a vraisemblable.
Or, enunciations can not be, by definition, explicated to a
conclusion: if I speak of an enunciation, it is no longer of it
that I speak but of an already enunciated enunciation which
has its own enunciation that I would never know how to enunciate.*[27]

The intersection of Heisenberg's uncertainty principle as formulated by Todorov in relation to the *vraisemblable* leads us
to another requisite of metonymy and Yuppie pathos: **repetition without origin**, (or, the impossibility of identity . . .)[28]

Yuppies evince a frantic aimless search to be "where it's at"
in order to be. If metaphor for Lacan is linked to being, metonymy is linked to its lack. This can be read in Yuppie food
preference: "Dream whipped mashed potatoes are the Yuppie
Everest because, for the time being, they're **there**." Being
there is culinarily expressed in two preferences that rely on
the senses or emotions. As Lévi-Strauss would have it, Yuppies prefer the hot and the old: pepper/nostalgia. These two
groups can be combined as, for example, with **false** Cajun
and Tex-Mex *manqué*, as foods that never were. Nostalgia
isn't what it used to be. "Yuppies need a burning sensation
to break through and remind them of the present or where
they ate last night."[29] But pepper not only reminds some Yuppies of where they were/are but of absent parents: New York
Yups were given spicy Chinese takeout so parents could attend rent strike meetings or lengthy European films! Szechuan
cuisine, or the absent mother . . .

Yet this facetious example strangely echoes Genette's insight
about Proustian involuntary memory and the key role of metonymy. The chain of metaphorical association is fueled by
metonymic contagion. "If the initial droplet of involuntary memory is of the order of metaphor, the edifice of memory is entirely
metonymic."[30] Proust's "sensation—signal" becomes an
equivalent of the context that it is associated with.[31] Metonymic displacement is also important for the Proustian theme.
Swann frequents a restaurant with the same name as the
street where his love object, Odette, lives: *La Perouse. "Hom-
onyie sur metonymie.* Such is the rhetoric of desire."[32] Hom-
onymia/metonymia and the conflation of desire with restaurants concludes this section as it does the first.

III. Metonymy in Foucault: *Usage* as *Verschiebung*

Critical reception of Foucault's last volumes affirm the status of **Usage/Souci** as a displacement (*Verschiebung*) from the earlier works. This veering off from a projected line of inquiry and a publishing timetable has been duly noted by Foucault in the extraordinary introduction to **Usage**. A theoretical displacement was necessary to understand (1) the forms of discourse which articulate knowledge; (2) the manifestations of power; (3) the constitution of the subject. "A theoretical displacement seemed necessary to me in order to analyze what had been designated as the progress of knowledge."[33] We have a long justification of theoretical displacement as necessary to philosophic enterprise. ("But what then is philosophy today—I mean philosophic activity if it is not the critical work of thought on itself?"[34]) How and just how far is it possible to think as an Other? Yet Foucault's account of his detour is described in a language of *Verschiebung* and frenzy curiously reminiscent of Lacan on metonymy: his curiosity to "*se dé-prendre*"—detach oneself, come loose, **melt** (does this limpid prose reveal a new "soft" Foucault?); his willful *égarement/* wandering.[35] Compare his rumination with Lacan: "The fury (*acharnement*) of knowledge isn't in its accumulation but in the way it enables us to wander; in the frenzy of the knowing subject."[36] Lacan similarly links metonymy, frenzy and knowledge/desire in "The Insistence of the Letter":[37]

And the enigmas which desire seems to pose for a 'natural philosophy'— its frenzy mocking the abyss of the infinite. The secret collusion by which it obscures the pleasure of knowing and of joyful domination, these amounting to nothing more than the derangement of the instincts that comes from being caught on the rails—eternally stretching forth towards the desire for something else—of metonymy.

If the preface to **Usage** can be read as a metadiscourse on displacement/metonymy, it also represents a displacement of them for Foucault's *oeuvre*. Both **Usage/Souci** are displacements of the power-knowledge nexus to a genealogy of the desiring subject. Domination and discipline gives way to a genealogy of ethics for ". . . the first exercise over individuals is their own confessional interpretation of themselves."[38] The power-knowledge nexus is replaced by techniques of the self or modes of subjection. From power to aesthetics, normalization to asceticism, subtle shifts are in evidence (all consonant with the figure of metonymy). Deviance is replaced by quantitative notions (e.g., moderation, *hubris,* excess) or a shift in focus (e.g.: activity/passivity, non-reciprocity, decorum). The displacement from questions of proscription/transgression to that of contiguity, propinquity, and measure will be seen to echo Lacan on metonymy. Indeed, Foucault's apparent trajectory from **Discipline and Punish** to **History of Sexuality** volume one to **Usage/Souci** is perfectly resumed by the Lacanian formula for metonymy:[39]

SAVOIR—————>DOMINER ————>JOUISSANCE

KNOWLEDGE——>DOMINATION ————>"BLISS"

Moreover, metonymy will function on three levels central to Foucault's problematic: (1) as a figure of desire; (2) as a figure of power/ideology; (3) as a figure that articulates the relationship between the subject and truth. Rather than reading **Usage** according to the paradoxical formulation of bio-power as proposed by Dreyfus and Rabinow, we will see Foucault's shift in relation to a coherent figurative strategy of metonymy.

Diogenes Laertius reports that he had the habit of doing everything in public: eating and fucking. And he reasoned thus: if it is not wrong to eat, it wouldn't be any more wrong to eat in public.[40]

Diogenes' discourse on eating out accompanies an equally insolent gesture: "When he needed to satisfy his sexual appetite, he relieved himself on the public square."[41] Yet Diogenes' comportment is less a provocation than a limit case of *chresis aphrodesion*: a privileged reduction of cause-effect to an instantaneous moment of pure need and its satisfaction. Antitheses at Xenophon's **Banquet** presents a similar economy: "If I were incited by some amorous desire, I would satisfy myself with the first one who came along . . ." [42] **Aphrodesia** are no more and no less than the satisfaction of an need. Nothing shameful, prohibitive or particularly transgressive about it. Rather all is a question of economy/immediacy. What is valorized is the most simple satisfaction of alimentary and sexual needs. For, if aphrodesia are regulated by need, the objective isn't to do away with pleasure, it is a question of maintaining it and ". . . maintaining it through need which would arouse desire."[43] And if Diogenes gives us food for thought it is in his wistfulness. What a shame that we can't find ways to feed ourselves as directly as masturbation satisfies our sexual appetite! Wouldn't it be great, Diogenes apostrophizes, ". . . if we could just rub (*frotter*) our stomachs to appease hunger?" Yet Foucault suggests (in a rare humorous aside) that masturbation does have its culinary counterpart—that is, in raw meat.[44] If Diogenes is a limit case for Foucault, then for our purposes he also figures as more than an *hors d'oeuvre*. For Diogenes' gesture cannot be interpreted apart from its inscription in a political system that sought to keep aphrodesia in the dark, in private. And so it will be with the *regime*, a word that in French signifies both diet and a form of government that we will center our discussion of metonymy in **Usage**.

Let us focus on *aphrodesia/chresis* as kinds of subjectivizing practice that most exemplify the shift from transgression/interdiction to measure/timing.[45] For it would appear that the only ethical faults possible in the world described in **Usage** are those of quantity (immoderation) or position. Indeed, aphrodesia aren't envisioned *en bloc* as an activity but as a question of place, frequency and context: "a strategy of measure and moment, quality and opportunity." The diet/regime is a fundamental category of the aphrodesia comprising exercise (*ponoi*), food (*sitia*), drink (*pota*), sleep (*hupnoi*), and sex (*aphrodesia*). The domain of the regimes is canonical and measured.[46] For the regime has as its objective the elimination of excess. Immorality of pleasures, Aristotle notes in the **Nicomachean Ethics**, is one of exaggeration and excess. Hyperathleticism is one of the examples cited of taking excessive care of the body.[47] The goal of the regime is to establish a "just measure" between the order of the body and the order of ethics.[48] The question of temperance (*sophrosune*) is a concern of moderation but also and equally of appropriateness: "The temperate one isn't one without desire but he who desires with moderation, not more than is needed nor when it isn't appropriate."[49] Again we note that it is not a binary opposition between the permitted and the forbidden, but rather an oscillation between **more and less**. "It isn't a question of fixing for once and for all the 'business days' (*jours ouvrables*) of sexual pleasure: but rather of calculating the opportune moments and the appropriate frequency."[50]

Questions of circumstance are important even when they are formed on analogy. The "high season" (*haute saison*) for sex is different for men and women. Women are "cold and wet" while men are "hot and dry". Thus the moment of *venerea* for women is summer, men find their just measure in winter.[51] It is interesting to note that these two passages evince a figurative flourish which is highly unusual in these volumes and that both of these moments ("high season/banking days") are figures of speech that only make sense in relation to the calendar and diachrony. Yet the calendar isn't an imperative for Foucault, it is strategic: "The calendar isn't to be read as a set of imperative recipes but as strategic principles that one adapts."

Technè as problems of context are inscribed in the diet as *kairos* (opportune moments).[52] The diet links seasons or times of the day. *Diététique* is a question of time as *Economique* is the maintenance of a structural relation (i.e. the household, matrimony).[53]

diane
rubenstein

The regime of Diocles is recounted by Foucault as a "*veritable emploi du temps*".[54] Sleep is broken down into number of hours, time of the day, the quality of the bed, its hardness, etc. Ethical prescripts are eminently situational or in other words metonymic and non-universal.

Position is another contextual consideration. For the negative sexual ethic *par excellence* is to be passive in regard to pleasure. Sexual pleasure is distinguished by two roles and two poles; value is accorded by position: subject/agent vs. object/patient. Maleness and femaleness is no longer a question of nature but of activity (or its lack). Active subjects are by definition measured and opportune.[55] It is the valorization of activity and not the nature of the love object that makes sex with boys a problem for the Greeks. The resolution of how one makes an active subject (citizen) from a former love object will be with recourse to a calibration of age. Unlike the timetables in **Discipline and Punish** which created a normalized individual, the Greek timetables are what allow for the possibility of a true subjectivity. If power produces knowledge in **Discipline and Punish**, in **Usage** schedules produce **ethics**. There is an even more startling formulation of an ethical question around a notion of diachrony: incest is just a problem of timing! Old sperm and young bodies don't mix. (Foucault appears to consider only father-daughter cases of incest.) Diachrony recalls the pleasure of memory. The goal of the aphrodesia, like the function of Proust's Madeleine, is to "find a pleasure worthy of memory. An accomplished moral subject has an exactly measured comportment . . . worthy of a long memory."[56]

IV. Tropes ᴙ'US

*One cannot help but be struck by the coincidence of this new version of power and the new version of desire proposed by Deleuze or Lyotard: no longer the absence or interdiction, but the **dispositif**, the positive dissemination of flux or intensities. This coincidence isn't accidental: it's simply that in Foucault power holds the place of desire. It is there as desire is with the others: always-already there, purged of all negativity, it is network . . . **it is contiquity diffracted to infinity**.[57] Jean Baudrillard, **Oublier Foucault (Forget Foucault)***

Baudrillard's **Oublier Foucault** underlines the difficulty of dissociating a discourse on power from a powerful discourse. Or, Foucault deploys the same technologies of power as those he describes. The promise of uniting reality and truth, making politics legible in discourse ("Power is no longer of the despotic order of the forbidden and the law, but of the objective order of the real")[58] is coupled with a writing style of just measure:

"The meaning never exceeds what it says within it . . . No vertigo, no fantasy, no void, no rhetoric."[59] One might similarly argue for "just measure" in Foucault's recent volumes. One cannot underestimate the importance of metonymy in situating the "break" with the earlier works. Rather than see a shift from considerations of power to those of desire coupled with a writing style that is continually realistic, I prefer to link desire, power and truth effect in the figure of metonymy and read Foucault against Lacan's "Insistence of the Letter." In other words, where Baudrillard sees power and desire as the same **problem**, I see Baudrillard's reading as metaleptic (a kind of metonymy that substitutes cause for effect and effect for cause). Power and desire appear to be the same problem because they are the same figure—metonymy. Moreover, metonymy is an active principle in the double rhetorical question that Lacan raises *à propos* of the figures used by his patients (periphrasis, hyperbation, ellipsis, denial, digression, irony labelled by Quintillian as catechresis, litotes . . .):[60]

Can one really see these as mere figures of speech when it is the figures themselves which are the active principles of the rhetoric of the discourse which the patient in fact utters?

Metonymy as Desire

As we noted in our previous discussion of Yuppie grazing rites: "Man's desire is a metonymy." The impossibility of the signifier from ever crossing the bar creates an incessant *renvoi* (dismissal, postponement, reference, return, **belch**) to anterior and future signifiers. For Lacan, man is engaged in a meaningful game between metaphor and metonymy "up to and including the active edge which splits my desire between a refusal of meaning and a lack of being."[61] The frenzy, derangement or more literally the de-railing of the instincts characterizes the incessant *renvoi* as the "**desire for something else.**" Barthes writes: "To be with the one I love and to think of something else. This is how I do my best work."[62] Metonymy as a figure of desire is inextricably bound up with, enmeshed in, and chain-linked to the path of the Lacanian signifier.

But desire can also be situated in Jakobson's reductive bipolar schema. If, as Genette notes, the emphasis on contiguity reduces metonymy to its spatial aspect,[63] the play of figures is then reduced even further to considerations of a physical or sensorial nature. Thus Foucault's "Grecian formula" which inserts desire in relation to acts or pleasure is all too appropriate:[64]

actes————————————plaisir————————————(desir)

92 Acts are underscored, the sensorial is secondary and desire is in brackets.

diane
rubenstein

Metonymy as a figure of ideology/power

But the focus on contiguity has similarly obscured the nature of metonymy as a figure of power which articulates ideology. Recent linguistic interpretations of metonymy have focused on its ideological purport. For what distinguishes metonymy from metaphor is the position of the **intermediary term**. In metaphor the intermediary term is contained (*englobé*); in metonymy it is *englobante*/containing.[65]

Take the Pascalian metaphor (**please**): "Man is a thinking reed. *L'homme est un roseau pensant.*" (One is struck by its similarity to Lacan's example of metaphor from Victor Hugo's **Booz Endormi**: "His sheaves were neither miserly nor spiteful."[66] Why is metaphor's promise of meaning always phallo(go) centric?)

The intermediary term of the Pascalian metaphor is fragility which is shared by both man and reed and situated between them:

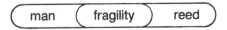

The intermediary term is **denotative**.

Metonymy, in contrast, is a figure of **ideological connotation.**[67]

The contiguity between the terms of departure and arrival inflate (*gonfler*) the role of the intermediary term. Fages chooses champagne as an example which designates both the wine and the province of its origin:

Indeed, because the metonymy is a combinative (and a combinatory works on the principle of gearing/meshing—*engrenage*—of contiguous signs) the bar can't be crossed or the chain would break. There is no longer the superposition as a metaphor, but a kind of contiguity which suggest more than a chain of signifiers, but *debordément* (extension beyond, a jut out over, overwhelming, outflanking, untucking) and "*position englobante*" as a result of ideological connotation. This new interpretation permits "apparent crossings of the bar, pseudo crossings of the unconscious signifier."[68] It is this latter interpretation which privileges it for Foucault as it enables the figure to show the servitude inherent in its presentation. Metonymy is a figure which lends itself to truth under oppression.[69]

Let us resume this discussion of the englobalizing capability of metonymy with an overtly political and (we will see) a highly motivated example: Washington, which functions as a metonym for the city and the government (and which more recently has functioned as the metonym for metonymy when we seek a political example to replace those ill-fated ships with sails.)

Washington

city   government

Truth and Tropes

*What one ought to say is: I am not, wherever I am, the plaything of my thought: I think of what I am wherever I don't think I am thinking. This two-faced mystery is linked to the fact that the truth can be evoked only in that dimension of alibi which all realism in creative works takes its virtue from **metonymy**.*

J. Lacan[70]

*When in 1784 Kant asked, "**Was heisst Aufklarung**?" he meant, What's going on just now? What's happening to us? What, in this work, this period, this precise moment in which we are living? Or, in other words: what are we as **Aufklarer**, as part of the Enlightenment? Compare this with the Cartesian question: "Who am I?" I, as a unique but universal and unhistorical subject? I, for Descartes is **anyone**, **anywhere** at **any** moment.*

M. Foucault[71]

Both Foucault and Lacan reformulate the Cartesian *cogito*. Kant's question "What are we?" is reinscribed in the metonymic style of two volumes that form part of his project to write a history of the present through a Grecian turn. Lacan assails the mirage of the *cogito* by the questioning of the place that the subject occupies as the subject of a signifier. The question of being for Lacan as for Foucault's Greek subjects, is a question of contiguity, for: "Being isn't posed before the subject but **in its place** . . . as one poses a problem with a pen."[72] The questions of place, subjectivity and language intersect. Lacan laments: "Is what thinks in my place then another I? Who then is this other to whom I am more attached than myself?"[73] The self's radical eccentricity to itself is revealed

94

only with the emergence of language. Radzinski, commenting on Lacan, notes that the constitution of the desiring subject is less a philosophical *renvoi* (reference, postponement, dismissal, **belch**) than it is an effect of a philosophical enunciation.[74] If the self can only be a subject of/for knowledge with the emergence of language, one is tempted to reformulate Foucault's pronouncements on sex: **in tropes there is truth**.

Sound familiar? Foucault, of course, was not the first to acknowledge the gesture of tropes as truth. Nietzsche assimilated truth to tropes in "Truth and Lying in an Ultramoral Sense": "What therefore is truth? **A mobile army** of metaphors, metonymies, anthropomorphisms . . . " But this paradoxical formulation is, to cite Deman's felicitous expression, "more familiar than understood."[75] It is with this ambivalent and disorienting structure of truth as a mobile army that we will conclude.

The notion that truth is a mobile army is strange. For, as Deman notes, if we say truth is an army (with the connotation of "collectivity")[76] of tropes, we are implying that truth is relational: the articulation of a subject (truth) by a predicate ("army of tropes") and moreover, linking a few predicates whose principle of articulation isn't identical. In this reading to say that truth is an army of tropes is to say that it is possible to enunciate a few propositions on a single subject, and Deman is to the point in seeing nothing particularly destructive about this. It is when we turn to the peculiar inventory of tropological examples that disorientation ensues and the militia appear. For anthropomorphism is not simply a trope. It is an identification on the level of substance (referent, signified). In other words, it crosses the bar to the referent, and history appears in the place of the *renvoi*. For anthropomorphism is a figure that takes something for something else in a manner that implies a logical progression; it substitutes something for something else whose constitution is **assumed as given**. "Anthropomorphism freezes the infinite chain of transformations/ tropological propositions into a single assertion that excludes all others. It is no longer a proposition but a proper name."[77] Therefore tropes such as metaphor, metonymy and anthropomorphism are mutually exclusive. Truth then will be sustained by two imcompatible assertions (Truth is a set of propositions; truth is a proper name-noun.) While it may be possible, Deman argues, to cross the bar that takes trope to name, "it is impossible once this barrier is crossed, to return to truth. For truth is a trope, tropes engender norms or value." This value (or ideology) is no longer true. "It's true that tropes are producers of ideologies that are no longer true."[78]

This leads to the notion of truth as a mobile army. All tropes are mobile; indeed one deploys tropes and we all talk about a figurative **strategy**. Yet "army" is at least as symptomatic as "anthropomorphism." For Nietzsche does not envision truth as an army in the sense of having a commander-in-chief who enlists tropes in the battle against error. "Whoever battles the truth battles stupidity, not error." To call truth an army is simply to reinscribe power within knowledge: "To call truth an army is to imply that their effectivity isn't due to judgment, but to power. Tropes being neither true nor false but both at once." As Deman so cogently notes, what makes a good army different from a good cause is effectivity ("an appropriately economic use of force/*puissance*"). To pose the question of truth as trope **in a military context** is truly disorganizing. This would have truth not only as power/force, but a power independent of epistemic determinations. "To call truth an army of tropes thus reaffirms its epistemic power as well as its strategic power." This unpeaceful coexistance of two modes of power (epistemic and strategic) underlines Nietzsche's story as it will, I hope, outflank (*déborder*) our concluding example.

Rambo: Truth as Trope as Troop

Sylvester Stallone defends his film as a right-wing fantasy with a figurative strategy that is as disorienting as Nietzsche's:[79]

So it's a right wing fantsy, like Valley Forge. They did it their way, too, against the British. **No one told them from Washington how to fight**. *This is the point: frustrated Americans try to recapture some glory.* **The vets were told wrong**. *The people who pushed the wrong buttons all took a powder. The vets got the raw deal and were left holding the bag. What Rambo is saying is that if they could fight again, it would be different.*

Truth, like Rambo, is a mobile army of tropes, metonymies and anthropomorphisms.[80] Stallone's elocution is a jumble of mixed metaphors, displaced commercials (Valley Forge as Burger King: "They did it their way") which produces a canonical metonym: Washington, denoting place and connoting government. The problem of Vietnam is one of metonymy: desire to rewrite/refight (or at least to win the war in the movies), frustration from this impossibility of desire coupled with nostalgia, which for Lacan is charged with metonymy. The desire for glory similarly underlines the importance of the other's recognition: "Recognition of desire is bound up with desire of recognition." Indeed, the problem of Vietnam follows the trajectory desire/impossibility, frustration/nostalgia, glory/*cogito, cogito*/enunciation. For the problem of Vietnam, its truth, is above all a problem of enunciation: **The vets were told wrong!**

diane
rubenstein

The problem of enunciation which is the truth of Vietnam becomes literalized now in Stallone's own concrete problem of
enunciation. A series of apparently mixed metaphors ensues:

*The people who pushed the wrong buttons all took a powder/
The vets got the raw deal and were left holding the bag.*

But what appears to be a metaphor, as Genette noted in his
reading of Proust, is an effect of metonymic concatenation.
Wrong buttons are contiguous to nuclear war which reduces
everything to a powder (concatenation of cause and effect).
"Raw deal . . . bag" could also work (as we saw with Foucault
on Diogenes) as a vulgar concatenation of raw (meat) and
(scum or douche) bag. After all, gentility is not one of Rambo's
virtues. But the ideological purport of these apparent, seeming
(*vraisemblable*) mixed metaphors is only realized when we
remember the conflation that characterizes metonymy as "*englobante*": The concatenation due to the textual contiguity of
"wrong button/raw deal" connects nuclear war and machis-
mo. In other words, peace (piece) with honor.

Yet Stallone's discourse contains more than a metonymy and
a series of mixed metaphors fueled by concatenation. Washington is an anthropomorphism; especially in the context of
Valley Forge, **Washington is a proper name**. And it is this as
it was with Nietzsche which is so profoundly disturbing. For
as anthropomorphism crosses the bar to referent, it evinces
a historical pathos. As anthropomorphism "freezes the infinite
chain of transformations," it forbids retrospective propositions. The possibility of Rambo serving a legitimate therapeutic
function as Professor Graff would have it ("Pictures like **Rambo** allow us to think it through 20 years later without the
casuality lists before us")[81] are exploded by Stallone's an-
thropomorphic *lapsus*. If not for anthropomorphism, the truth
of Vietnam might be told. If not for Washington, Rambo might
be true. There is always a danger in crossing the bar. And
that danger is precisely that you cannot rewrite history.

If Rambo's **epistemological** status is disorienting, the **strategic** power of Rambo can still be read in an equally uneasy
and inevitable metonym: **Ronbo** posters which place Reagan's
head atop Stallone's body with the subtext: "Reagan: No
man, no law, no war can stop him." The posters, like the
Pershing missiles, are to be deployed internationally. The only
hope would reside in that aporia between Ronbo as metonym
and the truth of Ronbo as anthropomorphism, which might
alert us that the problem of Rambo isn't one of judgment, but
of **power** (raised symptomatically by the juxtaposition of metaphor, metonymy and especially, anthropomorphism).

We recall Nietzsche's dictum with a certain poignancy: language, unlike Rambo, aims but misses.

University of Wisconsin

NOTES

1. Jan Hoffman, "The Feeding Habits of Yuppies," **Village Voice** (April 16, 1985). I would like to thank Libby Ames for bringing this article to my attention.

2. Gerard Genette, "La Rhétorique Restreinte," **Figures III** (Paris: Seuil, 1972) 34. An English translation of this aricle is included in Genette, **Figures of Literary Discourse**, Columbia University Press. All translations, unless otherwise noted, are my own. Jean Baptiste Fages gives the following definition of metonymy: from the Greek *metonumia*, change of name. It is a procedure through which one expresses effect by cause, container by contained, or the whole by the part. Fages, **Comprendre Jacques Lacan** (Paris: Privat, 1971) 39. Jakobson defines metonymy as "a substitution of signifiers that have a relation of contiguity." Roman Jakobson "Two Types of Aphasia and Two Types of Aphasic Disturbances" in Jakobson and Halle **Fundamentals of Language** (Hague: Mouton and Co., 1956).

3. Genette 27.

4. **Voice** 15.

5. Genette 27, 28, 34.

6. Fages 44. Lacan accepts Jakobson's definition as a substitution based on contiguity. For example, in the metonym "The White House spoke today" the White House serves as a container for the President (contained). Its formula is represented by: $f(S \ldots S') S+S$ (-)s. The function of metonymy poses a signifier, S White House which is in a relation of contiguity with President (S) as an anterior signifier that it replaces. This operation refers to a relation between metonymic signifers and signified which will be represented as S/s but the bar between S and s cannot be crossed, therefore the sign (-). If signification is produced by metonymy it is because of the connection of two signifiers. Metonymy is always an apparent nonsense. (The White House doesn't speak, although one might wonder if Larry Speakes, the Presidential spokesman, exemplifies a newer interpretation of metonymy which would include pseudo-crossings of the bar.) A certain constitutive absence is inscribed in metonymy—a partial signifier, which arouses a frenetic desire, a *renvoi* from one signifier to another. Metaphor, in contrast, is situated where sense is produced out of nonsense. In addition, for Lacan, the metonymic structure is between signifiers "which alone permits the elision in which the signifier inserts its lack of being into the object relation, using the reverberating character of meaning to invest it with the desire aimed at the very lack it supports." J. Lacan "The Insistence of the Letter in the Unconscious," **The Structuralists From Marx to Levi-Strauss** (Garden City, Anchor, 1972) 310.

7. Lacan 305: "In the case of *Verschiebung*, displacement, the German term is closer to the idea of that veering off of meaning that we see in metonymy, and which from its first appearance in Freud is described as the main method by which the unconscious gets by censorship."

8. Lacan 299.

diane
rubenstein

9. Michel Foucault, "The Subject and Power" in Hubert Dreyfus and Paul Rabinow, **Michel Foucault: Beyond Structuralism and Hermeneutics** (Chicago: Chicago University Press, 1982) 210.

10. Dreyfus 229.

11. **Voice** 11–12.

12. **Voice** 11.

13. Dreyfus 231.

14. **Voice** 13.

15. Dreyfus 253. On the connection between the deep self and sex and truth see also Michel Foucault's introduction to **Herculine Barbin, Being the Recently Discovered Memoirs of a Nineteenth Century Hermaphrodite** (N.Y.: Vintage, 1980) xi, as well as **History of Sexuality** Vol. I, page 69.

16. Dreyfus 235.

17. Edmund White, "The Emperor of the Mind," **Vogue** (Oct. 1984).

18. Jakobson 77, 70, 69.

19. A. Radzinski, "Lacan/Saussure: Les Contours Théoriques d'une Rencontre," **Langages** (Mars 85, no. 77). Radzinski situates appropriation as one of Lacan's strategies of "*Détournement, déplacement, amalgame*" in other words, displacement and concatenation.

20. **Voice** 14.

21. **Voice** 14.

22. **Voice** 14.

23. Tzvetan Todorov, "Du vraisemblable que l'on ne saurait éviter," **Communications** 11: 1968.

24. Roland Barthes, "L'effet du Reel," **Communications** 11: 1968. The use of metonymic detail to subvert the real is perversely manipulated in a later work of Barthes: **Sade, Fourier, Loyola**, especially in his "biographemes"—Fourier's predilection for perfect melons, pastries known as mirlitons, and the company of lesbians. See also Mark Seltzer, "Reading Cells," for a discussion of metonymy in Zola, **Diacritics** (Spring 1984).

25. Jackobson 78.

26. Genette 27.

27. Todorov 18.

28. Lacan 322 and 292: "It is in the chain of signifiers that the meaning insists but that none of its elements consists in the meaning of which it is at the moment capable." For repetition without origin and the difference between metaphor-metonymy see also J. F. Lyotard, **Economie Libidinale** (Paris: Seuil, 1974) 298.

29. **Voice** 12–13.

30. Genette, "Metonymie chez Proust", **Figures** III, 61.

31. Genette "Metonymy" 56–58.

99

32. Genette "Metonymy" 58–59.

33. Michel Foucault, **Usage des Plaisirs** (Paris: Gallimard, 1984) 12.

34. Foucault, **Usage** 15.

35. Foucault, **Usage** 14–15.

36. Foucault, **Usage** 14.

37. Lacan 313.

38. Leo Bersani, "Sexuality and Aesthetics," **October** 28 (Spring 1984)
27.

39. Fages, 45.

40. Foucault, **Usage** 65.

41. Foucault, **Usage** 64.

42. Foucault, **Usage** 65.

43. Foucault, **Usage** 66.

44. Foucault, **Usage** 65: *"Il aurait essayé de manger de la viande crue."*

45. Foucault, **Usage** 274. See also 130.

46. Foucault, **Usage** 115.

47. Foucault, **Usage** 118.

48. Foucault, **Usage** 116.

49. Foucault, **Usage** 81.

50. Foucault, **Usage** 132.

51. **Usage** 131; Jean Baudrillard **Oublier Foucault** (Paris: Galilée, 1977)
11.

52. Foucault **Usage** 73.

53. Where incest is a question of the *"bon moment"* for Foucault (**Usage**
69–70) for Barthes, incest is a surprise of vocabulary: "Thus transgression
appears as a nominative surprise; to posit that the son or husband (depending upon whether the father Noirceuil, sodomizes his son or is sodom-
ized by him) fills Sade with the same wonder as that which seizes the
Proustian narrator when he discovers that Guermantes' Way and Swann's
Way come together: incest, like time recaptured, is only a surprise of vocabulary. **Sade, Fourier, Loyola**, Richard Miller trans., (N.Y.: Hill and Wang,
1976) 139.

54. Foucault **Usage** 118.

55. Foucault **Usage** 56–7, 99. Compare this with Barthes on activity/pas-
sivity and the problem of homosexuality in **Roland Barthes**: "Virile/nonvirile
rules over the entire doxa . . . Homosexuality a transgressive practice in
Arab countries reproduces within itself . . . the purest paradigm imaginable
of active/passive, of possessor/possessed, buggerer/buggeree . . . in such
countries, then, the alterative is pure, systematic: it knows no neutral or
complex term . . . this alternative is neutralized by *petit bourgeois* boys
"Who need a discourse both sadistic and anal and clear **butt**ressed on
meaning (emphasis mine); they want a pure paradigm of meaning and of

sex, without a leak, without a flaw, without any overflow toward the margins." Richard Howard, trans. (N.Y.: Hill and Wang, 1977) 133.

56. Foucault **Usage** 65.

57. Baudrillard 22.

58. Baudrillard 10.

59. Baudrillard 11.

60. Lacan 315.

61. Lacan 312.

62. Barthes **The Pleasure of the Text** 24.

63. Genette "Rhetoric" 34, 28.

64. Dreyfus 243.

65. Fages 61.

66. Lacan 301.

67. Fages 62.

68. Fages 63.

69. Lacan 299.

70. Lacan 312.

71. Dreyfus 216.

72. Lacan 310.

73. Lacan 318.

74. Radzinski 132.

75. Paul Deman "Anthropomorphism et trope dans la poésie lyrique" **Poétique** (Dec 1984).

76. Deman 132.

77. Deman 133.

78. Deman 133.

79. **Time** (international edition) June 24, 1985: 53.

80. Lacan also speaks of troop movements when he recounts the joke about the two Jews going to Lvov. Lacan 320.

81. **Time** (international edition) June 24, 1985: 53.

thomas flynn

foucault as parrhesiast:
his last course at the collège de france
(1984)

His first class began three weeks later than announced. The large hall in which Bergson used to lecture was filled to overflowing, students sitting in the aisles and on the floor around the dias, a battery of speakers for tape recorders crowding the desk at which Foucault was to sit. He entered the room precisely on the hour, sat at the desk and assumed the pose he would often maintain throughout the course—forehead leaning lightly on his upraised arm, eyes cast down on the manuscript before him: "I apologize for the delay in meeting the class, but I was sick." Then, as if to confound the skeptics accustomed to professorial ploys, he paused, looked out at the auditors and insisted: "I really was!" I doubt that any of us present that first day has failed to reflect on those words in light of his tragic death scarcely four months later. Not once in the intervening lectures did he give any indication of failing strength or flagging spirit. Indeed, if it is true that he knew he was going to die in the near future, his *sangfroid* or better Stoic indifference is amazing. And yet, given his admiration for the classical Greek and Roman thinkers, especially the Sophists and the Cynics, to have acted otherwise would have been out of character.

The topic for this term's lectures was the same as the previous year, namely, the practice of truth-telling (*parrésia, le franc parler*) in the ancient Greek and Roman worlds. But whereas his earlier treatment had focused on parrhesia as a political virtue, you told the prince the truth even if it cost you your head, his subject this semester was truth-telling as a moral virtue, you admitted the truth even if it cost you your self-image.

All such truth-telling involves the presence of an other, even admitting the truth about oneself. In the latter case this other may be another philosopher, a teacher, friend, lover or sage. The qualification of the other for the Greeks was not institutional authority as with the Christian Church, nor was it a professional ability or competence as would later be required of psychoanalysts. What was expected in the case of telling the truth about oneself was that the other likewise be a truth-teller, not a flatterer or a coward. (This was the condition of the parrhesiastic "contract" established between the two parties.)[1] A relationship of **power** (subjectification and control) is thereby constituted between the subject and the other by telling the truth. One becomes a confessing subject who is likewise subject to the judgment of the other. This raises questions about the mode of "*veridiction*" involved as well as the practice and the techniques of self government at work here, issues Foucault began to treat in his **History of Sexuality**.

In what follows I wish to discuss three central themes treated in these lectures, namely, the characteristics of the parrhesiast in contrast with other truth-tellers (I), the pivotal role of Plato's Socrates in the transformtion of parrhesia from a political to a moral virtue (II), and the practice of the ancient Cynics as exemplars of this new, ethical parrhesia (III). I shall conclude with several observations about the significance of these lectures for the development of Foucault's thought (IV).

I

The parrhesiast in fourth-century Greece has to meet certain prior conditions. Of course, he had to speak the truth, but this truth could not be merely a *de facto* verity, a mere coincidence of speech with fact. He had to really believe it himself and to manifest that belief. Moreover, in speaking the truth, the parrhesiast had to run a personal risk before the other to whom he spoke. There was risk of violence at the hand of the interlocutor. Traditionally, the messenger always ran the risk of learning the truth as well. So parrhesia entailed the courage of the truth on both sides of the ledger, but especially on the part of the speaker.

The rhetorician, in Foucault's view, was the open contrary of the parrhesiast. He did not have to meet these prior conditions to enter into discourse. For example, he did not have to believe what he said. The characteristic link in his case was not with what he said but with the audience to whom he said it. Moreover, unlike the parrhesiast, he was a professional in classical society with a metier of his own.

But if all parrhesiasts are truth-tellers, not all truth-tellers are parrhesiasts. To bring this point home, Foucault distinguishes four basic modalities of saying the truth, namely, those of the prophet, the sage, the teacher-technician and the parrhesiast. Each respectively is concerned with truth as destiny, as being, as *technē* and as *ethos*.

The prophet tells the truth not in his own name, as does the parrhesiast, but as mediator between the principal speaker and his auditors. Unlike the parrhesiast, who speaks about the present and does so clearly and directly, the prophet mediates the present and the future and does so in words that require a certain interpretation because typically they cover even as they unveil what is hidden.

Speaking in his own name, the sage is distinct from the prophet. Indeed, holding his wisdom in himself, he feels no need to express it at all and, if questioned, may simply remain silent like Heraclitus. He speaks of what is, of the being of the world and of things, and does so in the form of general principles. In this he differs from the parrhesiast, who is obliged to speak and who speaks of the individual and of the present situation.

The teacher-technician, Socrates, for example, in a Platonic dialogue, possesses *technē*, a skill learned by apprenticeship and capable of being transmitted to others. Unlike the sage, he is traditionally obliged to transmit his truth-knowledge. But he runs no risk in doing so. He depends on a common tie with his students that unites and binds, whereas the word of the parrhesiast divides, even if it may bind and cure. In contrast with the prophet, the teacher seeks to be utterly clear and unambiguous.

Foucault notes that in antiquity these four modalities were well defined and institutionalized. But they were not mutually exclusive social roles. The same person, again Socrates, for example, could play each of them, though he was depicted by Plato primarily as a parrhesiast.

Anticipating his larger project of the history of the production of truth,[2] Foucault observes, in a kind of tantalizing aside suggesting areas for future research, that these four modes of speaking the truth have received different emphases in diverse "regimes of truth," i.e., in different disciplines and historical societies. The history of philosophy, for example, has focused more on the sage and the parrhesiast than on the prophet or the teacher-technician. Consequently, a "philosophic truth- telling" has emerged in the Western philosophical tradition that deals primarily with being and *ethos*. The Medieval Christian world stressed the prophetic and the parrhesiastic modalities, especially with the rise of preaching orders that commonly addressed eschatological themes. The university tradition focused on the sage and the teacher. Political, revolutionary discourse emphasized the prophetic and the parrhesiastic. In fact, later in the course, Foucault will again mention this revival of the parrhesiastic modality among romantic revolutionaries and bohemians in 19th-century Europe. This example of his "politics of truth" is obviously one he favored. Finally, the discourse of science, he claims, was in the tradition of the parrhesiast. Although Foucault did not develop this thesis here, it implies that science belongs with politics and ethics rather than with metaphysics, with doing and the particular rather than with being and the general, in its mode of truth-telling. How this applies to the social sciences, which violate the Aristotelian ban on "science of the singular" by emphasis on case studies, is a theme of his archaeology of the human sciences in **The Order of Things**.[3]

II

Foucault assigns an ambiguous role to Plato's Socrates in the evolution of parrésia similar to that he plays in the transformation of sexual ethic in the same period. Specifically, in the history of "sexuality" it was Plato's work that supported both the metaphysically oriented concern for love "in its very being" and the more practically motivated aesthetic of "care of the soul."[4] The former inspired the application of a moral code against which to measure the uses of pleasure and an asceticism linked with access to truth. The latter, with its ideal of self-mastery, served as touchstone for an entire "culture of the self" which flowered among the educated class in the Hellenistic era.

Similarly, Plato's work signals both the older tradition of parrhesia within the *polis* and the transformation of truth-telling from politics to ethics. It is a fruitful ambiguity in his use of "*parrésia*" that contributes to this transformation.

Politically, *parrésia* was a right of the citizen. One of the most painful aspects of exile, according to Euripides, was loss of this right to speak one's mind. It left the stranger little more than a slave as far as governance of the city was concerned.[5] But "democratic" parrhesia was criticized by the aristocrats in fourth-century Athens because it gave freedom of speech to the masses, that is, to those who judged in view of the desires of the crowd, not in terms of what was best for the *polis*. Their opposition was not only an expression of class interest; it revealed a perceived structural incompatibility between parrhesia and democracy that challenged Greek political thought for generations. One can recognize the plight of Socrates before the *demos* as Plato's example of the dangers of such false parrhesia. He criticizes it directly in Book VIII of the **Republic** [557a-b]. But the transitional nature of Plato's position lies in his continued respect for parrhesia as a personal attribute of character despite a basic distrust of "democratic" parrhesia. The focus of parrhesia is no longer the citizens nor even the *politeia* but the soul (*psyché*), especially that of the prince which, because it is educable, is capable of moral transformation to the benefit of all. The objective of parrhesia is the formation of a certain way of acting, of an ethos of the individual.

This emergence of parrhesia as transformative of the soul, Foucault notes, introduces three irreducible but interrelated poles into philosophical discourse which will remain in place to this day, namely, the dimensions of *alétheia* (forms of saying the truth), of *politeia* (structures and rules of governance), and of *éthos* (principles and norms of moral activity; guide for a stylistic of life). Elsewhere, Foucault has argued that these constitute three possible domains of genealogical analysis, each focusing on a distinctive form of self constitution, namely, constitution as subject of knowledge, as subject acting on others, and as moral agent.[6] It is significant, however, that the genealogy of *alétheia* in his earlier works, specifically, **The Birth of the Clinic** and **The Order of Things**, considered the subject chiefly as the "object" of authoritative knowledge. In these last lectures, Foucault addresses the subject as the "agent" of truth-telling, as actively entering into the "game" of the true and the false. Moreover, this genealogy is primarily ethical, even as it explicitly refers to the domain of "veridiction" and implicitly to that of power. In fact, Foucault now urges, philosophical discourse distinguishes itself from the exclusively political or moral by its necessary reference to all three poles.

So if we consider the four modes of truth-telling in terms of properly philosophical discourse, something like the following schema emerges: prophecy seeks to collapse *alétheia, politeia* and *éthos* as it focuses on the production of truth concerning the future; wisdom claims to think their basic unity; *techne* tries to define their irreducibility and distinctiveness, that is, their heterogeneity; parrhesia seeks the political conditions and the ethical differences at work in the question of true discourse, in other words, it underscores the impossibility of thinking any one without thinking all three poles, while insisting on their irreducible distinctness.

One can see in Foucault's gloss on his own remarks about Plato's contribution to the moral dimension of parrhesia a direct reference to what we may call the Foucaultian "triangle" of **knowledge, power and subjectivation** operative in his most recent works.[7] We may say that for Foucault these three dimensions of any question in their ensemble and mutual relationships mark the matter as properly philosophical. The philosopher is a parrhesiast in this new, ethical sense.

If Plato consigned to the Sophists the "political" dimension of the very concept of truth (thereby ignoring the power which was being exercised by his "contemplative" view of truth), he contributed mightily to both the knowledge and the subjectivation aspects of any philosophical question. It is to this last aspect, the relation of truth-telling to the constitution of the (moral) subject, that we must turn to appreciate Plato's contribution to the shift from political to moral parrhesia in the Western tradition. Foucault's analysis centers on three dialogues.

In the **Apology**, Socrates argues as a parrhesiast. He speaks at the risk of his life, but not like a political parrhesiast, not like Solon, for example, facing the threat of Pisistratus. Rather than address the people as the law-giver or the doctor of a sick state, he speaks like a father or an older brother. He has renounced politics in order to tell a truth of another kind, that of philosophy to which the divine voice calls him. This new veridiction has three characteristics. With regard to the god, it involves undertaking an *elenchus*: rather than interpreting the message and awaiting the effects of the god's pronouncement, Socrates subjects the oracle to inquiry and proof in the field of truth. Next, the form of his verification is a **probing of souls**, their confrontation in terms of knowledge and ignorance. Thirdly, this enterprise incurs the **hostility** of those questioned, thus confirming the parrhesiastic nature of the undertaking. The mission of Socrates as ethical parrhesiast, is not to do politics but to awaken others to be concerned with themselves (*phronésis*), with their truth (*alétheia*) and with their soul (*psyché*). Together these form the basis of an ethics, a way of comporting one self with regard to the true. Thus, Foucault sees Socrates's famous daimonic prohibition as drawing a line that separated two types of parrhesia: the political and the ethical.

Still, in the **Apology** Socrates exercises the three other forms of veridiction, albeit in a manner distinctly his own. He is dealing with a divine prophesy, though one which he transforms from the field of the real to that of the true. As a sage, he suffers the reputation of impiously seeking to know about the heaven above and the earth beneath, but in fact his concern is not the being of things nor the order of the world but the soul. Finally he is a teacher, although, unlike the sophists, he accepts no money and runs great personal risk for his effort. So he distinguishes himself not only from the prophet, the sage and the teacher, but from the political parrhesiast as well. This new, Socratic parrhesia is properly **philosophical** in that it is concerned with practical reason (*phronésis*), with truth and with the soul—sides of the Foucaultian "triangle" we noted above. It is the aspect of "care of the soul" (*epimeleia*) which serves as a vehicle for the emergence in two early dialogues, the **Alcibiades Major** and the **Laches**.[8]

According to Foucault, each dialogue initiates a line of philosophical inquiry that will perdure in Western thought. The **Alcibiades**, although its context is still political parrhesia, discusses the education of a young man based on the principle of care of the soul that implies the possibility and the need for the soul to contemplate itself. This "metaphysics of the soul" (*psyché*) that places a primacy on *logos* in the project of self mastery and builds on the distinction between the world of the changeable and the "other" world of the changeless grounds the care of the soul which Socrates later enjoins on his fellow citizens in the **Apology**.

But it is the **Laches** which is of greater interest to Foucault. Here he sees another mode of veridiction emerge which is concerned more with life (*bios*) than with the soul and which views philosophy more as a "testing of life" (*l'épreuve de la vie*) than as a knowledge of the soul. No doubt, the standard Platonic arguments for a metaphysics of the soul are enunciated in this dialogue as well. But Foucault hears another voice in counterpoint to the traditional *cantus firmus*. Its theme is "rendering an account of oneself" as the terminus of the parrhesiastic game that Socrates joins with his interlocutors. The account sought, however, is not an essence or form but a relation between one's self and the logos one proclaims; in other words, the **manner** in which one lives and has lived one's life.

An important transformation of Socratic parrhesia is taking place. His authority early in the dialogue derives, not from technical expertise (after the Platonic model of the craftsman or the navigator), but from the **harmony** that obtains between his *logos* and his *bios*, his doctrine and his life. What is at issue is not a "testing" of one's life once and for all but an on-going practice, a certain style of life. Socratic parrhesia now appears as asking one to give an account of oneself so as to lead one to care for oneself. But this care of oneself is not just the "care of the soul" of the **Alcibiades** and the **Apology**, namely, contemplation of the soul as a distinct reality. Rather, this alternative care of oneself denotes a manner of living as well as a self-knowledge of a quite different sort from the contemplative: it involves a practical proof, a testing of the manner of living and of truth-telling that yields a certain **form** to this rendering an account of oneself, a life-long examination that issues in a certain **style of existence**. In sum, the ambiguity of the Socratic principle of rendering an account of oneself (or, for that matter, of the interpretation of the Delphic injuction to know thyself) resulted in two distinct, if complementary, approaches to parrhesia, one which focused on a metaphysics of the soul, its essence or being, and another that led to a stylistic of life, an aesthetic of existence. Though the relationship between these two modes of veridiction is subtle and nuanced, Foucault argues that the metaphysics of the soul dominated philosophic discourse in the West.

He concludes that, while one can speak of an aesthetic of life (*bios*) in Greek thought (indeed, it is the aim of volumes two and three of his **History of Sexuality** to do so), this side of the parrhesiastic distinction has been eclipsed by the metaphysical, at least among philosophers. And yet a person's way of living, his "traces" in the eyes of his survivors, can be an object of aesthetic concern. The *bios* can be a beautiful work.

Yielding to his obvious preference for this latter form of care of the self, Foucault interjects the warning not to forget the aesthetic of existence in favor of concern for the beauty of things or even for the metaphysics of the soul. He allows that this was not a dominant theme in the thought of Socrates, that, in fact, one had to wait for Pindar and others for it to gain full attention. But his point is that this concern for a beautiful existence (*souci de l'existence belle*) was linked to concern for truth-telling by means of care of the self in the work of Socrates at the dawn of Western philosophy. The art of existence **is** truth-telling (*le dire vrai*). But developing this relation between the beautful life and truthtelling, a relation which is the "true life" (*la vraie vie*), Foucault concludes, is a matter he will leave for others.

III

In fact, Foucault did not leave entirely to others the task of fleshing out the relationship between the aesthetic of existence and the true life. It was the Cynics who afforded him the opportunity to consider this issue in a context characteristically free from theoretical encumbrances. The practice of the Cynics was one of the few exceptions to the general absence of the aesthetic of existence from the mainstream of philosophic discourse in the West.

The Cynic was characterized by friend and foe alike as a parrhesiast, indeed, as a kind of prophet of truth-telling. His deliberately unconventional lifestyle freed him for the task. In fact, the Cynics made of their lives a liturgy of truth-telling, carrying to the extreme the Socratic harmony described earlier. Foucault sees at the core of this movement the theme of **life as the scandal of truth**. It is in this "moral" guise that it penetrated Western thought.[9]

The Cynics' scheme of life is difficult to summarize theoretically. It is expressed and transmitted by stories, paradigmatic figures like Hercules and case histories. Because what is to be communicated is a way of life more than a doctrine, the philosophic hero becomes of prime importance and philosophic legend is common coin. (Foucault notes that this approach was considerably weakened once philosophy became the *métier* of professors and that the last such philosophic hero was probably Goethe's Faust: "Exit Faust and enter the revolutionary.")

The relation between truth-telling and the Cynics' way of life is forged by the concept of the "true life" (*aléthés bios*). It was the true life that the Cynics were transmitting by word and example. Foucault explains that *alétheia* in Greek philosophy assumed four guises: the true as the nonhidden; the true as what has no foreign admixture which would make it impure; the true as the correct, as conforming to a rule; and the true as what exists in identity and immutability, beyond all change. Accordingly, "true life" for Plato meant: one not dissembled with regard to its intentions or ends; a life without mixture of virtue and vice; a life of rectitude, lived in accord with norms and rules; one that escaped corruption or fall and hence one not divided in itself.

Foucault sees the Cynics' extreme, indeed scandalous, pursuit of the true life as an **inversion** of, a kind of carnivalesque grimace directed toward, the Platonic tradition. This, he believes, is the meaning of the Delphic Oracle's gnomic advice to Diogenes: "Change the value of the money." For the forms and habits of common life one must substitute the philosophers' principles, but **lived to the point of scandal**. Far from random grossness, the Cynics' practices challenged philosophers to live radically different lives from those conforming to the received wisdom of their contemporaries. For the Socratic "other world" they substituted an "other life," the truly philosophical life, the "true life."

Specifically, the Cynics' inversion of the true life entailed: 1) absence of dissemblance to the point of dramatization, their notorious "naturalism"; 2) lack of admixture of virtue and vice as exemplified in their poverty (an inversion of Stoic indifference), which led paradoxically to dependency, mendicancy and dishonor (*adoxia*); 3) rectitude understood as life according to the natural demands of animality, including the rejection of social conventions and taboos; and 4) self-possession and sovereignty pushed to the extreme of claiming a militant king-ship which fights against customs, institutions, personal pas-sions and vices to restore us to our natural state. The true life, the philosophic life, is one of mission, of service to others, as guides and "guard dogs" of all humankind, not just for members of an elite group. The universality of this mission, Foucault insists, is something new in classical philosophy.

The primary role which Foucault accords the Cynics in the history of philosophy is that of offering a major **alternative to Platonism**. By inverting the "true life" of the Platonists, Stoics and others, linking it with parrhesia as a style of living and with "care of the self" understood as the mission of challeng-ing the erroneous institutions, beliefs and practices of all peo-ple, the Cynics brought to the fore that other parrhesia intro-duced in Plato's **Laches** but neglected for the sake of a metaphysics of the soul and a theory of the other world, which charcterized the subsequent Platonic philosophical tradition.

If it is true, as Heidegger claims, that Western philosophy has forgotten Being in order to construct a kind of metaphysics, so, Foucault argues, has its neglect of "philosophical life" (the "true life," parrhesia as an aesthetic of existence) inclined it to see "truth" in primarily scientific terms. It is this Foucaultian moral that I wish to address in my concluding remarks.

IV

Foucault worked in the tradition of Cavaillès, Koyré, Bachelard and Canguilhem—philosophers of science whose approach was historical and decidedly neither platonic nor Cartesian.[10] What he added to their epistemological approach was a Nietz-schean sense of the power relationships at work in seemingly disinterested discourses as well as a certain linguistic turn in his theorizing. The latter abated in his later works but the former increased in scope and subtlety, joining the production of truth and the constitution of the moral subject as central themes and major instruments of analysis—what I have called the Foucaultian "triangle." But if these thinkers wrestled with the type of history suitable to scientific knowledge, Foucault's growing concern was with the "history" of reason itself: How did it happen that rationality in the West laid claim to a universal validity? What contingency lay at the base of such rationalistic necessity?[11]

Like his predecessors in the philosophy of science, he sees the "despotic Enlightenment" as the contingency at the center of this problem and he joins the Frankfurt School in urging that reason can have "the effect of emancipation only on the condition that it succeeds in freeing itself of itself."[12] But his interest in and respect for classical Greek culture will not allow him to stop (or to start) with the eighteenth century. As with his re-thinking of the history of sexuality, his "history" of reason leads him back to the first flowering of Western philosophy in fourth-century Athens. We must read the latest chapter in his history of the production of truth in terms of this anti-Enlightenment (and ultimately anti-Platonic) project. It carries a "moral" significance in that it is a liberation from the received norms of rationality and truth and to that extent it resembles Critical Theory to which it has often been compared.

But if Foucault's project of a history of truth and of reason as the vehicle of truth resembles the Frankfurt theorists' in what it decries, namely, a timeless, acontextual Reason that ignores its own values and interests, it differs markedly from their enterprise in what it fosters: not a historical Reason that unifies multiplicities in a developmental totality, but a plurality of counter-positions, of points of resistance, of styles of life—of "truths."

In pursuing this strategy, Foucault is aware of the risks he runs, risks defined chiefly in terms of the Reason he at base is questioning. First of all, there is the danger of burying one's own arguments in the sand of self-reference. This objection was leveled against him when he undertook to describe the epistemic grids that made "knowledge" possible within a series of discursive communities. His answer then as it would be now was that he is fully aware of the ground shifting under his own feet and that he merely wants to bring to our attention the contingency of our epistemic necessities, not to settle any issue (except perhaps that of absolute knowledge) once and for all.[13]

Of course, his opponents will counter that he loses critical purchase on whatever rationality he describes if the one he employs is itself under suspicion. While I believe that this traditional argument carries a certain plausibility, I think it misses the "flavor" of Foucault's claim. His is a skepticism more in line with Montaigne's "*Que sais-je*?" than with the obviously self-defeating form, "I can't be certain of anything." The subtle, questioning stance **casts suspicion**; it does not settle issues. But that is all Foucault intends. For in weakening our confidence in homogeneous reason and univocal truth, he has opened the door to new alternatives, other creativities, further "revolutions." Ethical parrhesia is one such alternative.

112 Although his last course does not refer explicitly to the "politics of truth," a theme of his genealogies of the carceral system and of sexuality, it does raise the issue of an "aesthetics of truth," continuing the topic of the aesthetics of existence raised in the second and third volumes of his history of sexuality. Again, the strategy is anti-Platonic and nominalistic. In a manner that suggests Bataille's Nietzschean reading of Hegel, Foucault is attempting to "crack open" the metaphysical notion of truth as ahistorical, unconditioned and one. He undertook this project indirectly in his archaeologies by historicizing the concept of reason and underscoring the breaks in epistemic conditions for nonformal sciences since the Renaissance and he addressed it explicitly in his genealogies of the power relationships at work in our social practices of punishment and sexual control. His objective was to show how entering into the "game" of the true and the false, whether by choice or chance, is in either case an exercise of power (domination, selectivity, entitlement and control) and in no way represents how things simply "have to be" (a Platonic cosmos).

The result is not epistemic anarchy. The proliferation of events and truths in Foucault's discourse is not without rhyme or reason. But these reasons are in the plural and the history of their appearance and demise can be charted, if not explained. Furthermore, as exercises of power, they are tactical and strategic; they must be read in terms of "how," "when" and Where," not "what" and "why," another inversion of Platonic values.

What I have termed Foucault's "aesthetics of truth" is his recent attempt to show that this multiplicity of events and truths is not without "rhyme." The Socratic parrhesia of harmony between one's *logos* and one's *bios* exemplifies such an aesthetic vision of truth. It is a truth one does or lives rather than says. And the living realizes a certain style, not a general rule or norm. Indeed, Foucault in this respect, doubtless *malgré-lui*, approaches Kierkegaard's concept of truth as subjectivity, despite the fact that he wants to sever the relationship between truth and the metaphysical subject.[14] Both philosophers are transgressing the limits imposed by a "scientific" concept of truth.

In addition to furthering his notion of an aesthetics of truth that extends his earlier remarks about an aesthetics of existence to the epistemic realm, Foucault's last lectures on parrhesia advance his thought in at least two other respects, namely, with regard to the "triangular" relationship of knowledge, power and subjectivation and the corresponding multiplicity of truths.

The question of the self constitution of the moral subject, which emerged in the history of sexuality, is complicated more than

clarified by reference to the moral parrhesiast. The issue centers on the **activity** of the subject in this process of self-
constitution. Is he/she the mere reflection of structural changes,
the simple nodal point of a multiplicity of impersonal relationships?

It is clear that Foucault continued to respect these "structuralist" concepts as he insisted that we "rethink the question
of the subject."[15]

But a lingering uneasiness remains if one believes such "passivity" suffices to account for the **self**-constitution of the moral
subject. No doubt a form of "historical a priori" makes certain
practices possible and excludes others. The courage of the
parrhesiast in face of possible violence, for example, may well
be encouraged and even taken for granted in a specific society
at a particular time. Messengers may be chosen for their moral
character as much as for their speed. But as Sartre reminded
the Marxist "economists," Flaubert may be a *petit bourgeois,*
but not all *petit bourgeois* are Flauberts. It is the question of
individual responsibility (a concept Foucault would historicize
as well) that assumes particular urgency in the context of moral
constitution. The excuse, "That's just the way I am!" carries
little weight in moral exchanges.

Foucault was facing an issue that many have regarded as the
Achilles' heel of Marxism and structuralism alike: the moral
implications of their theories of history and society. Do they
lead to a sterile amoralism, rendering inconsistent any viable
moral theory? Foucault's Nietzschean sympathies make him
hostile to moral norms as commonly conceived. But the increasing importance given the moral subject in his later work
as well as the interrelation of power and truth in its self constitution suggests that Foucault's account might leave room
for moral creativity in a way that eluded both Marx and the
structuralists.

The later volumes of his history of sexuality show admiration
for "ethics" understood as a style of comportment as distinguished from "morality" taken as a code or universal rule of
behavior. Although Foucault fails to distinguish the ethical from
the moral in his last lectures, it is clear that what we have
called the fruitful ambiguity of Plato's position refers to what
we may now term "moral" and "ethical" parrhesia. The former
denotes the moral virtue that perfects the soul of the philosopher who judges according to principles of being, not becoming. Ethical parrhesia refers to that harmonious life whose
style is an object of aesthetic delight, the beautiful-good (*kalon
kai agathon*). In Foucault's view, ethical parrhesia, like the art
of existence, is not bound to a metaphysical doctrine and so

can be championed by the Cynics and others concerned more with action than with being, even though we find its germ in Plato himself. The "ethical" parrhesiast thus emerges in a "tradition" from Diogenes to Nietzsche as an alternative, not a complement, to his moral counterpart.

If the triadic relationship of power, knowledge and subjectivation (self constitution) is essential to any properly philosophical analysis, as Foucault implies, then his own discussion of the ethical parrhesiast must be integrated into the larger issue of the production of "truth" (e.g., the "true life") as a form of self governance and social control. Although he does not address this point in these lectures, his interest in the aesthetics of existence and in ethics as "a very strong structure of existence without any relation with the juridical per se, with an authoritarian system, with a disciplinary structure,"[16] cannot exclude reference to the exercise of power, the practice of "veridiction" and the mode of subjectivation at work in every ethic or *techné* of life, including anarchism and aestheticism.

What is especially noteworthy about his last work is its increased focus on the subject, the agent and self-constitution, as if Foucault's polemic with the humanists had turned to dialogue. There is no indication that this was the case; he was not growing soft on subjectivism. But the groundwork was already in place for a genealogy of the modern subject. His histories of sexuality and of parrhesia take its first solid steps. The power-knowledge relationship of his earlier works is not only focused upon but is in turn translated by the relation of subjectivation in his later writings. Their precise interrelation is left unsettled. I speak of "translation" rather than "mediation" because of Foucault's hostility to Hegelian dialectic. But a three-fold circular (i.e., nontotalizing) reciprocity between truth, power and subjectivation seems to capture Foucault's position in his last works. In fact, in his 1980 Howison Lectures at the University of California, Berkeley, he insists that "if one wants to analyze the genealogy of the subject in Western societies, one has to take into account . . . the interaction between those two techniques of domination and of the self." Earlier in the same talk he reminds us that "all the practices by which the subject is defined and transformed are accompanied by the formation of certain types of knowledge."[17] So the threefold relation should be brought into play if one would escape the philosophy of the (meaning-giving) subject while charting the advent of the modern subject. Indeed, this genealogical charting is itself a form of liberation.

His final course also adds to the multiplicity of truths that appear once Platonic "truth" is broken apart. It is no great news that "truth" carries a variety of meanings. But seldom in the history of philosophy has such a concerted and sophisticated attack been waged on the commonly received notion that scientific truth is the paradigm, the standard for the rest. What his study of the parrhesiast adds to this discussion is an extended example of a fundamental, nonlogical form of truth.

But it also leaves us with the same dissatisfaction we felt with the account of "power" in his earlier works. In neither case are we given a definition of the term we are discussing. "Truth" remains as vague and elusive here as did "power" earlier. But in both cases the reason is the same. Foucault's "nominalist critique" of our history and culture requires that "truth" like "power" be conceived in the multiplicity of its occurrences, that it conform to no essence or *eidos*. Part of the force of genealogy as critique lies precisely in this nominalistic dismantling process.

Like his other histories, this one leaves us with a heightened sense of the contingency of our most prized necessities, the variability of our lodestar, the relativity of it all (if indeed "it all" existed). But rather than counsel some kind of transcendental (re)turn, as do Habermas and others, or propose a neopragmatist collapse of truth into power, knowing into doing, Foucault at this stage of his thought seems inclined to recommend a cautious skepticism with regard to utopian politics and a neostoic almost Camusian "pessimistic activism" in the face of ultimate meaninglessness.[18]

If, as he claims, the history of truth was his abiding interest, Foucault's last lectures were a kind of homecoming, not only because they brought into play his basic concepts and methods (an archaeology of knowledge, a genealogy of power and a problematization of truth and subjectivity), but because they directed these to the discourse and practice of an historical period and culture that held a special fascination for him. If his hard-fought battle against anthropologism kept him from idealizing Hellenic culture, he nonetheless admired and, indeed, practiced the kind of ethical parrhesia whose roots he uncovered in Plato but whose flower he savored among the "good" Cynics. For he too was taken with the crafted beauty of life, with the freedom of resistance, with the inverted, the fragmented, the aleatory. Indeed, there is something Greek about his tragic passing and about the philosophical torso he left behind. If Habermas failed to find in Foucault the unity of his theory and his practice,[19] it is perhaps because he overlooked the parrhesiast.

116

thomas flynn

NOTES

1. The nature of the parrhesiastic "contract" was discussed in Foucault's thus far unpublished lectures at The University of California, Berkeley the previous term but is only implicitly the subject of these lectures at the Collège.

2. Foucault was said to be writing a multi-volume history of the "production" of truth for a series edited by Paul Veyne. These lectures were clearly part of the project.

3. Michel Foucault, **The Order of Things** (New York: Vintage Books, 1983).

4. For a discussion of the Socrato-Platonic discourse on love, see Foucault's **The History of Sexuality**, vol. 2, **The Use of Pleasure**, trans. Robert Hurley (New York: Pantheon Books, 1985), pp. 229–246, and vol. 3, **Le Souci de soi** (Paris: Gallimard, 1984), pp. 57–85.

5. See Euripides, "The Phoenician Women," in **Orestes and Other Plays**, trans. Philip Vellacott (Harmondswoth, England: Penguin Books, 1972), lines 386–394.

6. See his Afterword (1983) to Hubert L. Dreyfus and Paul Rabinow, **Michel Foucault: Beyond Structuralism and Hermeneutics,** 2d ed. (Chicago: The University of Chicago Press, 1983), p. 237.

7. See my "Truth and Subjectivation in the Later Foucault," **The Journal of Philosophy** 82, No. 10 (October, 1985), pp. 531–540.

8. Foucault mentions his commentary on the **Alcibiades** in an interview in 1983. See Dreyfus and Rabinow, **Beyond Structuralism**, pp. 231 and 235.

9. Foucault lists three such points of penetration, namely, the Christian ascetical tradition to the extent that it suggested a form of life that publicly contradicted community norms and standards (e.g., mendicants and heretics in the middle ages); certain practices of the political militant, especially in the nineteenth century, such as unconventional communal life-styles exhibited as prophetic of a new age or as critical of the present one; and in the fine arts, the adoption of cynical themes and stances by satirists and comedians in the ancient world and later. Foucault singles out two ways in which modern art has been a vehicle for the cynical mode of being: the appearance of the "artist's life" (*la vie d'artiste*) at the end of the eighteenth century as a testimony that art itself can give form to life and that life belongs to the domain of art and, secondly, the "anti-cultural" stance of modern literary and plastic art both as often violently reducing the real to an elementary existence and as contesting even its own rules.

10. See Foucault's Introduction to the English translation of Georges Canguilhem, **On the Normal and the Pathological**, trans. Carolyn R. Fawcett (Dordrecht, Holland: Reidel, 1978). In fact, Foucault claims that Husserl's **Cartesian Meditations**, through which "phenomenology entered France," inspired two distinct readings: one, in the direction of a philosophy of the subject (Sartre and the existentialists), and another which returned to the founding principles of Husserl's thought (formalism and intuitionism). It was the latter that Cavaillès and others exploited (p. x).
For a glimpse of the early Foucault's own "existentialist" reading of phenomenology, see his Introduction to Ludwig Binswanger's **La Reve et l'existence**, translated by Forrest Williams and Jacob Needleman in **The Re-**

view of **Existential Psychology and Psychiatry**, Vol. XIX, No. 1, pp. 31–78.

11. Introduction to Canguilhem's **On the Normal**, p. xii.

12. **Ibid.** Critical as he was of facile appeals to origins and influences in intellectual history, Foucault elsewhere warns against seeing in the Enlightenment "**the** factor responsible for [in that case] totalitarianism." He points out to a group of professional historians that Europe for centuries has sustained "an extremely rich and complex relationship" with the Enlightenment which, borrowing a term from Canguilhem, he calls our most "current past" (*actuel passé*). (*Michelle Perrot, ed.*, **L'Impossible Prison** [Paris: Editions du Seuil, 1980], pp. 317–318.)

13. See **The Order of Things**, p. 384.

14. In fact, Kierkegaard's "subjectivity" like his "truth" is moral rather than metaphysical and, to that extent, resembles Foucault's concepts. Aside from the crucial contrast between these authors' views on subjectivity, another seemingly major difference concerns moral versus aesthetic "truth." It is unfortunate that Foucault was unable to develop his notion of an aesthetic of existence, which would have cast light on truth as harmonious living (ethical parrhesia) and related forms of truth. This, in turn, might have led others to notice aesthetic features in Kierkegaardian "truth as subjectivity."

15. Introduction to Canguilhem's **On the Normal**, p. xx.

16. Dreyfus and Rabinow, **Beyond Structuralism**, p. 235.

17. Foucault, "Truth and Subjectivity," Howison Lecture, Berkeley, California, October 20, 1980.

18. See Dreyfus and Rabinow, **Beyond Structuralism**, p. 232.

19. See Jürgen Habermas, "Taking Aim at the Heart of the Present," **University Publishing** 13 (Summer, 1984), pp. 5–6.

the works of
michel foucault
1954–1984

established by
James Bernauer
and
Thomas Keenan

Introductory Note. The greatest care has been taken to guarantee the completeness and accuracy of this bibliography. Section A lists all of his publications in their chronological order of composition (which in many cases is not their order of publication) when we have been able to establish such exactness. All English translations have also been identified. Section B lists miscellaneous materials. Section C takes note of the contents of studies which were conducted under his direction. The occasional symbols which we use refer either to Michel Foucault (MF) or to the principal words of his French titles (e.g., **AS** for **L'Archéologie du savoir**).

A) The Publications

1) **Maladie mentale et personnalité**. Paris: Presses Universitaires de France, 1954. Cf. #9 below.

2) "Introduction." To Ludwig Binswanger, **Le rêve et l'existence** ("Traum und Existenz"). Translated from the German by Jacqueline Verdeaux. Paris: Desclée de Brouwer, 1954, 9–128.

2ET) "Dream, Imagination, and Existence." Translated by Forrest Williams. **Review of Existential Psychology and Psychiatry** XIX, 1 (1984–1985) 29–78.

3) "La recherche scientifique et la psychologie." In **Des chercheurs francais s'interrogent**. Edited by Jean-Edouard Morère. Paris: Presses Universitaires de France, 1957, 171–201.

4) Translation into French with Daniel Rocher of Viktor von Weizsaecker, **Le cycle de la structure (Der Gestaltkreis)**. With a preface by Henry Ey. Paris: Desclée de Brouwer, 1958.

5) **Thèse complémentaire** for the doctorat ès lettres, University of Paris, Faculty of Letters and the Human Sciences, 1961. The Director of Studies: Jean Hyppolite. A typescript in two volumes that is available at the Bibliothèque Sorbonne, Paris. This thesis is an introduction to and translation, with notes, of Immanuel Kant, **Anthropologie (Anthropologie in pragmatischer Hinsicht)**.

Vol. I: Introduction, 128 pp. Vol. II: Translation and Notes, 347 pp. This volume was later published as **Anthropologie du point de vue pragmatique**. Paris: Vrin, 1964.

6) **Folie et déraison. Histoire de la folie à l'âge classique. Paris: Plon, 1961.** Reissued in an abridged form in 1964, Paris: Union Générale d'Editions. Reissued in original complete form as **Histoire de la folie à l'âge classique** (Paris: Gallimard, 1972) with different preface and two appendices: "La folie, l'absence d'oeuvre" (**La Table Ronde**, May, 1964) and "Mon corps, ce papier, ce feu" (**Paideia**, September, 1971). Reissued in the TEL collection without the appendices, Paris: Gallimard, 1978.

6ET) **Madness and Civilization**. Translated by Richard Howard. Introduction by José Barchilon. New York: Pantheon, 1965. The English version is a translation of the drastically abridged edition of 1964 with some slight additions from the original edition.

7) "La folie n'existe que dans une société." **Le Monde** 5135 (July 22, 1961) 9. An interview with Jean-Paul Weber.

8) Review of Alexander Koyre, **La révolution astronomique, Copernic, Kepler, Borelli**. La Nouvelle Revue Francaise 108 (December, 1961) 1123–1124.

james bernauer
and thomas
keenan

9) **Maladie mentale et psychologie**. Paris: Presses Universitaires de France, 1962, 1966. This is the revised edition of
#1 above with a totally different second part and conclusion.

9ET) **Mental Illness and Psychology**. Translated by Alan
Sheridan. New York: Harper and Row, 1976.

10) "Introduction." To **Rousseau juge de Jean-Jaques: Dialogues**. Paris: Librarie Armand Colin, 1962, vii–xxiv.

11) "Le 'non' du père." **Critique** 178 (March, 1962) 195–209.
An essay on Jean Laplanche's **Hölderlin et la question du
père**.

11ET) The Father's 'No'." In **Language, Counter-Memory,
Practice: Selected Essays and Interviews**. Edited by Donald
Bouchard. Translated by Donald Bouchard and Sherry Simon.
Ithaca: Cornell University Press, 1977, 68–86.

12) "Les déviations religieuses et le savoir médical." **Hérésies
et sociétés dans l'Europe pré-industrielle 11e–18e siè-
cles**. Communications et débats du Colloque de Royaumont
présentés par Jacques LeGoff. Paris: Mouton, 1968, 19- 29.
Foucault's presentation and the discussion which followed
took place at a conference from May 27–30, 1962.

13) "Le cycle des grenouilles." **La Nouvelle Revue Francaise**
114 (June, 1962) 1159–1160. Presentation of a text by Jean-
Pierre Brisset.

14) "Un si cruel savoir." **Critique** 182 (July, 1962) 597–611.
An essay on Claude Crébillon's **Les égarements du coeur
et de l'esprit** and J.A. Reveroni de Saint-Cyr, **Pauliska ou la
perversité moderne**.

15) "Dire et voir chez Raymond Roussel." **Lettre Ouverte** 4
(Summer, 1962) 38–51. In a modified version much of this
essay was later published as the first chapter of his volume
on Raymond Roussel. Cf. #18 below.

16) Translation into French of Leo Spitzer, "Art du langage et
linguistique." **Etudes de style**. Paris: Gallimard, 1962, 45–
78. Original English: "Linguistics and Literary History," in
Spitzer's **Linguistics and Literary History**. Princeton: Princeton University Press, 1948, 1–39.

17) **Naissance de la clinique. Une archéologie du regard médical**. Paris: Presses Universitaires de France, 1963. Revised edition published in 1972; cf. #87 below.

17ET) **The Birth of the Clinic: An Archaeology of Medical Perception**. Translated by Alan Sheridan Smith. New York: Pantheon, 1973. (A translation of revised edition with some exceptions).

18) **Raymond Roussel**. Paris: Gallimard, 1963.

18ET) **Death and the Labyrinth: The World of Raymond Roussel**. Translated by Charles Ruas, with an introduction by John Ashberry. New York: Doubleday and Company, 1986.

18A) "Le métamorphose et le labyrinthe." **La Nouvelle Revue Francaise** 124 (April, 1963) 638–661. This is chapter 5 of **Raymond Roussel**.

19) "Wächter über die Nacht der Menschen." In Hans Ludwig Spegg, ed., **Unterwegs mit Rolf Italiaander: Begegnungen, Betrachtungen, Bibliographie**. Hamburg: Freie Akademie der Kunst, 1963, 46–49.

20) "Préface à la transgression." **Critique** 195–196 (August-September, 1963) 751–769.

20ET) "A Preface to Transgression." In **Language, Counter-Memory, Practice**, 29–52.

21) "Un 'Fantastique de bibliothèque'." **Cahiers Renaud- Barrault** 59 (March 1967) 7–30. Republished as the introduction to G. Flaubert, **La tentation de Saint Antoine** with the title "La bibliothèque fantastique." Paris: Le Livre de Poche, 1971, 7–33. This essay, written in 1964, was originally published in a German translation by Anneliese Botond and used as the afterword to Flaubert, **Die Versuchung Des Heiligen Antonius**. Frankfurt: Insel, 1964, 217–251.

21ET) "Fantasia of the Library." In **Language, Counter-Memory, Practice**, 87–109.

22) "Débat sur le roman." **Tel Quel** 17 (Spring, 1964) 12–54. A discussion, held at Cérisy la Salle in September, 1963, directed by MF.

23) "Débat sur la poésie." **Tel Quel** 17 (Spring, 1964) 69- 82. A discussion, held at Cérisy la Salle in September, 1963, in which MF participated.

james bernauer
and thomas
keenan

24) "Le langage à l'infini." **Tel Quel** 15 (Autumn, 1963) 44-53.

24ET) "Language to Infinity." In **Language, Counter-Memory, Practice**, 53–67.

25) "Guetter le jour qui vient." **La Nouvelle Revue Francaise** 130 (October, 1963) 709–716. On Roger Laporte, **La Vielle**.

26) "Distance, aspect, origine." **Critique** 198 (November, 1963) 931–945.

27) "La prose d'Actéon." **La Nouvelle Revue Francaise** 135 (March, 1964) 444–459. On Pierre Klossowski.

28) "Le langage de l'espace." **Critique** 203 (April, 1964) 378-382.

29) "La folie, l'absence d'oeuvre." **La Table Ronde** 196 (May, 1964) 11–21. Republished as appendix to 1972 edition of **Histoire de la folie**, 575–582.

30) "Nietzsche, Freud, Marx." **Cahiers de Royaumont 6: Nietzsche**. Paris: Éditions de Minuit, 1967, 183–200. Conference, at which this paper was first delivered, took place in July, 1964.

30ET) "Nietzsche, Freud, Marx." Translated by Jon Anderson and Gary Hentzi. **Critical Texts** III,2 (Winter, 1986) 1–5. The discussion which followed Foucault's paper is not included in this version.

31) "Pourquoi réédite-t-on l'oeuvre de Raymond Roussel? un précurseur de notre littérature moderne." **Le Monde** 6097 (August 22, 1964) 9.

32) "Les mots qui saignent." **L'Express** 688 (Aug. 29, 1964) 21- 22. Review of Pierre Klossowski's translation of Virgil's **Aeneid**.

33) "Le Mallarmé de J.-P. Richard." **Annales** 19, No. 5 (Sept.-Oct., 1964) 996–1004. A review of Richard's **L'univers imaginaire de Mallarmé**.

34) "L'obligation d'écrire." **Arts** 980 (Nov. 11–17, 1964) 7. On Gérard de Nerval.

35) "Philosophie et psychologie." **Dossiers pédagogiques de la radio-télévision scolaire** 10 (February 15–27, 1965) 61–67. An interview conducted by A. Badiou.

36) **Les mots et les choses: une archéologie des sciences humaines**. Paris: Gallimard, 1966.

36ET) **The Order of Things: An Archaeology of the Human Sciences**. Unidentified collective translation. New York: Pantheon, 1971.

36A) "Les suivants." **Mercure de France** 1221–1222 (July-August 1965) 366–384. Identical to first chapter in **LMC**.

36B) "La prose du monde." **Diogène** 53 (Jan.-March, 1966) 20-41. This is a shortened version of the second chapter of **LMC**, in which it bears the same title. This was also published as "The Prose of the World." Translated by Victor Velen. **Diogènes** 53 (Spring, 1966) 17–37.

37) "L'arrière-fable." **L'arc** 29 (1966) 5–12. On Jules Verne.

38) "Entretien: Michel Foucault, 'les mots et les choses.'" **Les Lettres Francaises** 1125 (March 31, 1966) 3–4. An interview with Raymond Bellour. Republished in Bellour's **Le livre des autres**. Paris: Éditions de l'Herne, 1971, 135–144.

39) "Entretien." **La Quinzaine Littéraire** 5 (May 16, 1966) 14-15. An interview with Madeleine Chapsal.

40) Excerpt of a letter from MF to René Magritte, dated June 4, 1966, published in René Magritte, **Ecrits complets**, ed. by André Blavier. Paris: Flammarion, 1979, 521. Responds to letter from Magritte of May 23, 1966 which is included in **Ceci n'est pas une pipe** (cf. #53 below).

41) "L'homme, est-il mort: Un entretien avec Michel Foucault." **Arts et loisirs** 38 (June 15, 1966) 8–9. An interview with Claude Bonnefoy.

42) "La pensée du dehors." **Critique** 229 (June, 1966) 523–546. On Maurice Blanchot. Reprinted in book form: **La pensée du dehors**. Montpellier: Editions Fata Morgana, 1986.

james bernauer and thomas keenan

43) "Une histoire restée muette." **La Quinzaine Littéraire** 8 (July 1, 1966) 3–4. Review of Ernst Cassirer, **The Philosophy of the Enlightenment**.

44) "C'était un nageur entre deux mots." **Arts-loisirs** 54 (Oct. 5, 1966) 8–9. An interview with Claude Bonnefoy on André Breton.

45) "La pensée médicale." **Le concours médical** 88 (October 22, 1966) 6285–6286.

46) "Un archéologue des idées: Michel Foucault." **Synthèses** 245 (October, 1966) 45–49. An article on **LMC** by Jean-Michel Minon, with extensive quotations from an interview with MF.

47) "Introduction générale." To Friedrich Nietzsche, **Oeuvres philosophiques** Vol. 5: **Le gai savoir**. Texts and variations established by G. Colli and M. Montinari. Translated from the German by Pierre Klossowski. Paris: Gallimard, 1967, i-iv.

48) "Des espaces autres." **Architecture-Mouvement-Continuité** 5 (October 1984) 46–49. A lecture delivered on March 14, 1967.

48ET) "Of Other Spaces." Translated by Jay Miskowiec. **Diacritics** 16, 1 (Spring, 1986) 22–27.

49) "Deuxième entretien: Sur les facons d'écrire l'histoire." **Les Lettres Francaises** 1187 (June 15, 1967) 6–9. Second interview with Raymond Bellour. Republished in R. Bellour, **Le livre des autres**. Paris: Éditions de l'Herne, 1971, 189–207.

50) "Conversazione con Michel Foucault." **La Fiera Letteraria** 39 (Sept. 28, 1967). An interview conducted by P. Caruso and published in Italian. Republished in Caruso's **Conversazione con Levi-Strauss, Foucault, Lacan**. Milano: U. Mursia and Co., 1969, 91–131. There is a German translation by Walter Seitter published as "Gespräch mit Michel Foucault" in the collection of MF's writings: **Von der Subversion des Wissens**. Frankfurt: Ullstein, 1978, 7–31.

51) "Préface." To Antoine Arnaud and Pierre Nicolle, **Grammaire générale et raisonée**. Paris: Paulet, 1969, iii-xxvii.

51A) "La grammaire générale de Port Royal." **Langages** 7 (September, 1967) 7–15. An extract from #51.

52) "Les mots et les images." **Le Nouvel Observateur** 154 (Oct. 25, 1967) 49–50. A review of Irwin Panofsky's **Essais d'iconologie** and **Architecture Gothique et Pensée Scolastique**.

53) "Ceci n'est pas une pipe." **Les cahiers du chemin** 2 (Jan.15, 1968) 79–105. This essay on the painter René Magritte was reissued in an enlarged version as **Ceci n'est pas une pipe**. Montpellier: Scholies, Fata Morgana, 1973.

53ET) "Ceci n'est pas une pipe." Translated by Richard Howard. **October** 1 (Spring, 1976) 6–21. This translation was of the first edition but included some material from the enlarged version which was translated and edited by James Harkness, **This Is Not A Pipe** (Berkeley: University of California Press, 1982).

54) "Foucault répond à Sartre." **La Quinzaine Littéraire** 46 (March 1–15, 1968) 20–22. A radio interview with Jean-Pierre El Kabbach. The publication of this unedited transcript provoked a sharp reply from MF in the journal's following issue (March 15–31), 21: "Une mise au point de Michel Foucault."

55) "Réponse à une question." **Esprit** 371 (May, 1968) 850–874.

55ET) "History, Discourse and Discontinuity." Translated by Anthony Nazzaro. In **Salmagundi** 20 (Summer-Fall 1972) 225–248, and reissued in **Psychological Man**, edited by Robert Boyers. Harper: Colophon, 1975, 208–231. A revised translation by Colin Gordon was published as "Politics and the Study of Discourse." **Ideology and Consciousness** 3 (Spring, 1978) 7–26.

56) "Lettre de Michel Foucault à Jacques Proust." **La Pensée** 139 (May-June, 1968) 114–117. This comments on the discussion which the same journal published as "Entretiens sur Michel Foucault." **La Pensée** 137 (Feb., 1968) 3–37.

57) "Réponse au Cercle d'épistémologie." **Cahiers pour l'analyse** 9: **Généalogie des sciences** (Summer, 1968) 9–40. Excerpted as "Réponse au Cercle d'épistémologie." **Les Lettres Francaises** 1240 (July 10, 1968) 3–6.

james bernauer and thomas keenan

57ET) "On the Archaeology of the Sciences." **Theoretical Practice** 3-4 (Autumn, 1971) 108–127. An abridged translation with no translator identified.

58) **L'archéologie du savoir**. Paris: Gallimard, 1969.

58ET) **The Archaeology of Knowledge**. Translated by A. M. Sheridan Smith. New York: Harper Colophon, 1976.

59) "Médecins, juges et sorciers au XVIIe siècle." **Médecine de France** 200 (1969) 121–128.

60) "Jean Hyppolite (1907–1968)." **Revue de Métaphysique et de Morale** 74, 2 (April-June, 1969) 131–136. This was originally presented at the memorial session for Hyppolite on Jan. 19, 1969, at the Ecole Normale Supérieure.

61) "Ariane s'est pendue." **Le Nouvel Observateur** 229 (March 31, 1969) 36–37. A review of G. Deleuze's **Différence et répétition**.

62) "En bref: Précision." **Le Nouvel Observateur** 229 (March 31, 1969) 39. Correction to "Une petite histoire," **Le Nouvel Observateur** 227 (March 17, 1969) 43. On MF's being prevented from speaking in London.

63) "La naissance du monde." **Le Monde des livres** 7558 (May 3, 1969) viii. A conversation with Jean-Michel Palmier.

64) "Michel Foucault explique son dernier livre." **Magazine littéraire** 28 (April-May, 1969) 23–25. An interview on AS conducted by J.J. Brochier.

65) "Qu'est-ce qu'un auteur?" **Bulletin de la Société française de Philosophie** 63 (July-September 1969) 73–104. First presented as a lecture on Feb. 22, 1969. Foucault's remarks are followed by a discussion in which the following participated: Maurice de Gandillac, Lucien Goldmann, Jacques Lacan, Jean d'Ormesson, J. Ullmo, Jean Wahl.

65ET) "What Is An Author?" In **Language, Counter-Memory, Practice**, 113–138. Translation is slightly abridged and the discussion is omitted.

66) "La situation de Cuvier dans l'histoire de la biologie II." **Revue d'histoire des sciences et de leurs applications** XXIII,

1 (Jan.-March, 1970) 63–92. This presentation was made at a conference held May 30–31, 1969 and was followed by a discussion. Foucault also made comments on another paper delivered at the conference, that of Francois Dagonet, "La situation de Cuvier dans l'histoire de la biologie I" (presentation is on pp. 49–60 in the same issue of the journal with Foucault's comments on pp. 61–62).

66ET) "Cuvier's Position in the History of Biology." Translated by Felicity Edholm. **Critique of Anthropology** IV, 13–14 (Summer, 1979) 125–130.

67) Two letters from MF to Pierre Klossowski, dated July 3, 1969, and Winter, 1970–71, reproduced in **Cahiers pour un temps: Pierre Klossowski**. Paris: Centre Georges Pompidou, 1985, 85–88 and 89–90.

68) **L'ordre du discours**. Paris: Gallimard, 1971. MF's inaugural lecture at the Collège of France, Dec. 2, 1970.

68ET) "Orders of Discourse." Translated by Rupert Swyer, **Social Science Information** (April, 1971). Republished as "The Discourse on Language," an Appendix to ET of **L'archeologie du savoir** (cf. #58 above), 215–237.

69) "Présentation." To Georges Bataille, **Oeuvres Complètes I: Premiers Écrits** 1922–1940. Paris: Gallimard, 1970, 5–6.

70) "Sept propos sur le 7e ange." A preface to Jean-Pierre Brisset, **La grammaire logique**. Paris: Tchou, 1970, vii-xix. Republished in book form as **Sept propos sur le septième ange**. Montpellier: Editions Fata Morgana, 1986.

71) "Le piège de Vincennes." **Le Nouvel Observateur** 274 (Feb. 9, 1970) 33–35. An interview with Patrick Loriot.

72) "Il y aura scandale, mais . . ." **Le Nouvel Observateur** 304 (Sept. 7, 1970) 40. A note on Pierre Guyotat's **Eden, Eden, Eden**.

72ET) "Open Letter to Pierre Guyotat." Translated by Edouard Roditi. **Paris Exiles** 2 (1985) 25.

73) "Croître et multiplier." **Le Monde** 8037 (Nov. 15–16, 1970) 13. A review of Francois Jacob, **La logique du vivant**.

james bernauer
and thomas
keenan

74) "Theatrum Philosophicum." **Critique** 282 (November, 1970) 885- 908. This is a reflection on two books of Gilles Deleuze, **Différence et répétition** and **Logique du sens**.

74ET) "Theatrum Philosophicum." In **Language, Counter-Memory, Practice**, 165–196.

75) "Foreword." To the 1971 English edition of **LMC**. In **The Order of Things**, ix-xiv. Cf. #36 above.

76) "Entrevista com Michel Foucault." In **O homem e o discurso**. Rio de Janeiro: Tempo Brasileiro, 1971, 17–42. An interview conducted by Sergio P. Rouanet and J.G. Merquior. In Portuguese.

77) "Nietzsche, la généalogie, l'histoire." In **Hommage à Jean Hyppolite**. Paris: Presses Universitaires de France, 1971, 145-172.

77ET) "Nietzsche, Genealogy, History." In **Language, Counter-Memory, Practice**, 139–164.

78) "A Conversation with Michel Foucault." **Partisan Review** 38 (1971) 192–201. An interview by John Simon.

79) "Mon corps, ce papier, ce feu." **Paideia** (Sept., 1971). Reissued as Appendix to 1972 edition of **Historie de la folie**, 583–603. Cf. #6 above.

79ET) "My Body, this Paper, this Fire." Translated, with an introduction, by Geoff Bennington. **Oxford Literary Review** IV, 1 (Autumn, 1979) 5–28.

80) "Lettre." In **La Pensée** 159 (Sept.-Oct., 1971) 141–144. Foucault wrote in criticism of an article by Jean-Marc Pelorson, "Michel Foucault et l'Espagne." **La Pensée** 152 (August, 1970) 88–99.

81) "Human Nature: Justice versus Power." Published in **Reflexive Water: The Basic Concerns of Mankind**, edited by Fons Elders. London: Souvenir Press, 1974, 134–197. A discussion between MF and Noam Chomsky. Televised in November, 1971 by the Dutch Broadcasting Company and moderated by Fons Elders.

82) "Par delà le bien et le mal." **Actuel** 14 (Nov., 1971) 42–47. Interview with M.A. Burnier and P. Graine. Republished

with slight modifications as "Entretien." **C'est demain la veille.**
Paris: Seuil, 1973, 19–43.

82ET) "Revolutionary Action: 'Until Now.'" In **Language,
Counter-Memory, Practice**, 218–233.

83) "Monstrosities in Criticism." Translated by Robert J. Mat-
thews. **Diacritics** I, 1 (Fall, 1971) 57–60. This was written as
a reply to a review of **The Order of Things** by George Steiner:
"The mandarin of the hour—Michel Foucault." **The New York
Times Book Review** (Feb. 28, 1971) 8, 23–31.

84) "Foucault responds 2." **Diacritics** I, 2 (Winter, 1971) 60.
Foucault's response to Steiner's own reply to the preceding
entry. Steiner's piece was published as "Steiner Responds to
Foucault" **Diacritics** I, 2 (Winter, 1971) 59.

85) "Le discours de Toul." **Le Nouvel Observateur** 372 (December 27, 1971) 15.

86) "Histoire des systèmes de pensée." **Annuaire du Collège
de France** 71 (1971). Summary of the course given at the
Collège de France in 1971. Lecture: "La volonté de savoir."
Seminar: "Le fonctionnement du système pénal en France à
partir du XIXe siècle." Republished as Appendix in Angèle
Kremer-Marietti, **Michel Foucault** (Paris: Seghers, 1974) 195–
200.

86ET) "History of Systems of Thought." In **Language, Counter-Memory, Practice**, 199–204.

87) **Naissance de la clinique: Une archéologie du regard
médical.** Revised, second edition. Paris: Presses Universitaires de France, 1972.

87ET) Cf. #17 above.

88) "Préface." To new edition of **Histoire de la folie à l'âge
classique**. Paris: Gallimard, 1972, 7–9.

89) "Sur la justice populaire: Débat avec les maos." **Les
Temps Modernes** 310 (1972) 335–366. A discussion with
Philippe Gavi and Pierre Victor.

89ET) "On Popular Justice: A Discussion with Maoists."
Translated by John Mepham. In **Power/Knowledge: Selected**

james bernauer and thomas keenan

Interviews and Other Writings, 1972–1977, edited by Colin Gordon. New York: Pantheon, 1980, 1–36.

90) "Les intellectuels et le pouvoir." **L'arc** 49 (1972) 3–10. A conversation between MF and Gilles Deleuze which took place on March 4, 1972.

90ET) "Intellectuals and Power." In **Language, Counter-Memory, Practice**, 205–217.

91) "Michel Foucault on Attica." **Telos** 19 (1974) 154–161. An interview with John Simon in 1972.

92) "Table ronde." **Esprit** 413 (April-May, 1972) 678–703. A discussion, in which MF participated, on questions relating to social work and its clients. Other participants were: Jean-Marie Domenach, Jacques Donzelot, Jacques Julliard, Philippe Meyer, Rene Pucheu, Paul Thibaud, Jean-Rene Treanton, Paul Virilio.

93) "Gaston Bachelard, le philosophe et son ombre: Piéger sa propre culture." **Le Figaro** 1376 (Sept. 30, 1972) Litt. 16.

94) "Un dibattito Foucault-Preti." **Bimestre** 22–23 (Sept.-Dec. 1972) 1–4. A debate in Italian conducted by Michele Dzieduszycki.

95) "Médecine et lutte de classes." **La Nef** 49 (Oct.-Dec., 1972) 67–73. An edited round-table discussion between MF and members of the Health Information Group (Groupe Information Santé).

96) "Les deux morts de Pompidou." **Le Nouvel Observateur** 421 (Dec. 4, 1972) 56–57. Excerpts reprinted as "Deux calculs." **Le Monde** 8676 (Dec. 6, 1972) 20.

96ET) "The Guillotine Lives." Translated in abridged form by Paul Auster. **The New York Times** (April 8, 1973) section 4, p. 15.

97) "Histoire des systèmes de pensée." **Annuaire du Collège de France** 72 (1972) 283–286. A summary of the course given at the Collège de France in 1972. Lecture: "Théories et institutions pénales." Seminar: "Psychiatrie et pénalité au XIXe

131

siècle." Reprinted as appendix in Kremer-Marietti, **Michel Foucault**, 201–205.

98) "Préface." To Serge Livrozet, **De la prison à la révolte**. Paris: Mercure de France, 1973, 7–14.

99) "Présentation." To **Moi, Pierre Rivière, ayant égorgé ma mère, ma soeur et mon frère**. Edited by Michel Foucault. Paris: Gallimard, Julliard, 1973, 9–15.

99ET) "Foreword." To **I, Pierre Rivière, having slaughtered my mother, my sister and my brother**. Edited by Michel Foucault. Translated by Frank Jellinek. New York: Pantheon, 1975, vii-xiv.

99A) "Une crime fait pour être raconté." **Le Nouvel Observateur** 464 (October 1, 1973) 80–112. This article is an abbreviated version of his "Présentation" to **MPR** with excerpts from the memoir itself.

100) "Les meurtres qu'on raconte." **MPR**, 265–275.

100ET) "Tales of Murder." In **I, Pierre Rivière . . .** , 199–212.

101) "Pour une chronique de la mémoire ouvrière." **Libération** (Feb. 22, 1973) 6. A brief conversation with MF, a journalist and a worker named José.

102) "En guise de conclusion." **Le Nouvel Observateur** 435 (March 13, 1973) 92. A commentary on David Rosenhan, "Je me suis fait passer pour fou," 72–93.

103) "La force de fuir." **Derrière le Miroir** 202 (March, 1973) 1–8. On the artist Rebeyrolle.

104) "L'intellectuel sert à rassembler les idées, mais . . . 'son savoir est partiel par rapport au savoir ouvrier.'" **Libération** 16 (May 26, 1973) 2–3. A conversation between MF and a worker named José.

105) "Un nouveau journal?" **Zone des tempêtes** 2 (May-June, 1973) 3.

106) "A verdade e as formas juridicas." Translated into Portuguese by R. Machado. **Cadernos do P.U.C.**, 1974, 5–102.

james bernauer
and thomas
keenan

Five conferences by Foucault at the Catholic University of Rio de Janeiro on May 21–25, 1973. A discussion with MF is on 103–133.

107) "Entretien avec Michel Foucault: à propos de l'enfermement pénitentiaire." **Pro Justicia: Revue politique du droit** 3–4 (October, 1973) 5–14. An interview conducted by A. Krywin and F. Ringelheim.

108) "Gefängnisse und Gefängnisrevolten." **Dokumente: Zeitschrift für übernationale Zusammenarbeit** 29 (June 1973) 133–137. An interview conducted by Bodo Morawe.

109) "Convoqués à la P.J." **Le Nouvel Observateur** 468 (Oct. 29, 1973) 53. Written in collaboration with Alain Landau and Jean-Yves Petit.

110) "Entretien avec Gilles Deleuze, Felix Guattari." **Recherches** 13 (December, 1973) 27–31, 183–186.

111) "Histoire des systèmes de pensée." **Annuaire du Collège de France** 73 (1973) 255–267. A summary of the course given at the Collège de France in 1973. Lecture: "La société punitive." Seminar: "Pierre Rivière et ses oeuvres." Reprinted as appendix in Kremer-Marietti, **Michel Foucault**, 206–221.

112) "Les rayons noirs de Byzantios." **Le Nouvel Observateur** 483 (Feb. 11, 1974) 56–57. A review of **Trente dessins de Byzantios**.

113) "Sexualité et politique." **Combat** 9274 (April 27–28, 1974) 16.

114) "Entretien." **Cahiers du Cinéma** 251–252 (July-August, 1974) 5–15. An interview with Pascal Bonitzer and Serge Toubiana.

114ET) "Film and Popular Memory." Translated with some minor omissions by Martin Jordin. **Radical Philosophy** 11 (Summer, 1975) 24–29.

115) Three lectures on the history of medicine delivered at the Instituto de Medicina Social. Centro Biomédico, Universidad Estatal de Rio de Janeiro, Brazil, in October, 1974. "Crisis de

un Modelo en la medicina?'' **Revista Centroamericana de Ciencias de la Salud** 3 (Jan.-April, 1976) 197–210; ''El nacimiento de la mediciana social.'' **Ibid**. 6 (Jan.-April, 1977) 89–108; ''Incorporacion del hospital en la tecnologia moderna.'' **Ibid**. 10 (May-August, 1978) 93–104.

116) ''Table ronde sur l'expertise psychiatrique.'' **Actes: Cahiers d'action juridique** 5–6 (Dec. 1974-Jan. 1975). Reprinted in **Actes: Délinquances et ordre** (Paris: Maspero, 1978) 213–228. Other participants were Y. Bastie, A. Bompart, Diederichs, F. Domenach, P. Gay, J. Hassoun, J. Lafon, C. Marechal, P. Sphyras, F. Tirlocq. MF's interventions collected and republished as ''L'expertise psychiatrique.'' **Actes** 54: La gouvernementalité (Summer, 1986) 68.

117) ''Histoire des systèmes de pensée.'' **Annuaire du Collège de France** 74 (1974) 293–300. A summary of the course given at the Collège de France in 1974. Lecture: ''Le pouvoir psychiatrique.'' Seminar: ''Explication des textes médicaux et juridiques du XIX siècle.''

117A) A longer version of this text was later published as ''La casa della follia.'' Translated by C. Tarroni. In Franco Basaglia and Franca Basaglia-Ongaro, ed., **Crimini di Pace**. Torino: Einaudi, 1975, 151–169. The original complete French text was then published in Basaglia and Basaglia-Ongaro, ed., **Les Criminels de paix: Recherches sur les intellectuels et leurs techniques comme préposés à l'oppression**. Translated by Bernard Fréminville. Paris: Presses Universitaires de France, 1980, 145- 160.

118) **Surveiller et punir: Naissance de la prison**. Paris: Gallimard, 1975.

118ET) **Discipline and Punish: The Birth of the Prison**. Translated by Alan Sheridan. New York: Pantheon, 1977.

118A) ''La naissance des prisons.'' **Le Nouvel Observateur** 536 (Feb. 17, 1975) 69–86. This article is made up of excerpts from **SP**.

119) ''La peinture photogénique.'' An introduction to an exhibition of paintings by Fromanger: **Fromanger: Le désir est partout**. Paris: Galérie Jeanne Bucher, 1975. (10 pages, no pagination).

134

120) ''Préface.'' To Bruce Jackson, **Leurs Prisons**. Paris: Plon, 1975, i-vi.

james bernauer
and thomas
keenan

121) "Un pompier vend la mèche." **Le Nouvel Observateur** 531 (Jan. 13, 1975) 56–57. A review of Jean-Jacques Lubrina, **Enfer des Pompiers**.

122) "Des supplices aux cellules." **Le Monde** 9363 (Feb. 21, 1975) 16. An interview with MF conducted by Roger Pol Droit.

122ET) "Michel Foucault on the Role of Prisons." **The New York Times** (Aug. 5, 1975) 31. Excerpts translated by Leonard Mayhew.

123) "Sur la sellette." **Les nouvelles littéraires** 2477 (March 17, 1975) 3. An interview conducted by Jean-Louis Ezine.

123ET) "An Interview with Michel Foucault." Translated by Renée Morel. **History of the Present** 1 (Feb., 1985) 2–3, 14.

124) "Entretien sur la prison." **Magazine littéraire** 101 (June, 1975) 27–33. An interview conducted by J.J. Brochier.

124ET) "Prison Talk: an interview with Michel Foucault." Translated by Colin Gordon. **Radical Philosophy** 16 (Spring, 1977) 10–15. Republished in **Power/Knowledge**, 37–54.

125) "Pouvoir et corps." A June interview with MF in **Quel corps?** 2 (1975). Reissued in a collection of texts from the review and published as **Quel corps?** Paris: Francois Maspero, 1978, 27–35.

125ET) "Body/Power." In **Power/Knowledge**, 55–62. Translated by Colin Gordon.

126) "Foucault, passe-frontières de la philosophie." **Le Monde** (Sept. 6, 1986). An interview conducted by Roger-Pol Droit on June 20, 1975.

127) "La machine à penser s'est-elle detraquée?" **Le Monde Diplomatique** 256 (July, 1975) 18–21. Quotes MF, among others, in an inquiry into "a crisis of thought?," conducted by Maurice Maschino.

128) "Aller à Madrid." **Libération** 538 (Sept. 24, 1975) 1, 7. An interview conducted by Pierre Benoit concerning a delegation of seven French intellectuals, including MF, expelled from Madrid while denouncing death sentences imposed on anti-Franco militants.

129) "Faire les fous: Réflexions sur **Histoire de Paul.**" **Le Monde** 9559 (Oct. 16, 1975) 17. On the film by René Feret.

130) "À propos de Marguerite Duras." **Cahiers Renaud Barrault** 89 (October, 1975) 8–22. A conversation between MF and Hélène Cixous.

131) "Sade, sergent du sexe." **Cinématographe** 16 (Dec., 1975- Jan., 1976) 3–5. Interview conducted by Gérard Dupont.

132) "Histoire des systèmes de pensée." **Annuaire du Collège de France** 75 (1975) 335–339. A summary of the course given at the Collège de France in 1975. Lecture: "Les anormaux." Seminar: "L'expertise médico-légale en matiere psychiatrique."

133) **Histoire de la sexualité I: La volonté de savoir**. Paris: Gallimard, 1976.

133ET) **The History of Sexuality I: An Introduction**. Translated by Robert Hurley. New York: Pantheon Books, 1978.

134) "Les têtes de la politique." A preface to **En attendant le grand soir**, a book of sketches by Wiaz. Paris: Denoël, 1976, 7- 12.

135) "Un mort inacceptable." A preface to Bernard Cuau, **L'affaire Mirval ou Comment le récit abolit le crime**. Paris: Les presses d'aujourd'hui, 1976, vii-xi.

136) "La politique de la santé au XVIIIe siècle." The introduction to Part I, "L'Institution hospitaliere au XVIIIe siècle," of a three part study done under the direction of MF and published as **Généalogie des équipements de normalisation: Les équipements sanitaires**. Fontenay-sur-Bois: Centre d'Études, de Recherches et de Formation Institutionelles (CERFI), 1976, 1–11.

136ET) "The Politics of Health in the Eighteenth Century." Translated by Colin Gordon. In **Power/Knowledge**, 166–182.

137) "La crisis de la medicina o la crisis de la antimedicina." **Education medica y salud** 10, 2 (1976) 152–170.

138) "Sur **Histoire de Paul**." **Cahiers du Cinéma** 262–263 (January, 1976) 63–65. A conversation between MF and René Féret.

James bernauer
and thomas
keenan

139) "Questions à Michel Foucault sur la géographie." **Hérodote** 1 (Jan.-March, 1976) 71–85.

139ET) "Questions on Geography." Translated by Colin Gordon. In **Power/Knowledge**, 63–77.

140) "Crimes et châtiments en U.R.S.S. et ailleurs." **Le Nouvel Observateur** 585 (Jan. 26, 1976) 34–37. An interview with K.S. Karol.

140ET) "The Politics of Crime." A translation of large excerpts by Mollie Horwitz. **Partisan Review** 43 (1976) 453–459.

141) "Corso del 7 gennaio 1976," and "Corso del 14 gennaio 1976." In **Microfisica del Potere**. Edited by Alessandro Fontana and Pasquale Pasquino. Torino: Einaudi, 1977, 163–177, 179–194. Italian translation of two lectures, unpublished in France, which were delivered in January, 1976 at the Collège de France.

141ET) "Two Lectures." Translated by Kate Soper. In **Power/Knowledge**, 78–108.

142) "L'extension sociale de la norme." **Politique hebdo** 212 (March, 1976) 14–16. An interview, with P. Werner, on Szasz's **Fabriquer la folie**.

143) "Sorcellerie et folie." **Le Monde** 9720 (April 23, 1976) 18. A conversation with MF conducted by Roland Jaccard on Thomas Szasz's **Fabriquer la folie**.

144) "Intervista a Michel Foucault." An interview in June, 1976, conducted by Alessandro Fontana and Pasquale Pasquino. It serves as an introduction to their **Microfisica del Potere**, 3–28. Cf. #141 above for full entry.

144ET) "Truth and Power." Translated by Colin Gordon. In **Power/Knowledge**, 109–133.

144A) This interview was released in French as "Vérité et pouvoir." **L'Arc** 70 (1977) 16–26. Excerpts had appeared earlier as "La fonction politique de l'intellectuel." **Politique hebdo** 247 (Nov. 29, 1976) 31–33. An English translation of the latter was made by Colin Gordon and published as "The Political Function of the Intellectual." **Radical Philosophy** 17 (Summer, 1977) 12–14.

145) "Des questions de Michel Foucault à **Hérodote**." **Hérodote** 3 (July-Sept., 1976) 9–10. Foucault's questions were

replied to in the same journal, issue #6 (April-June, 1977) 7–30.

146) "Bio-histoire et bio-politique." **Le Monde** 9869 (Oct. 17–18, 1976) 5. Remarks on J. Ruffie's **De la biologie à la culture**.

147) "L'Occident et la vérité du sexe." **Le Monde** 9885 (Nov. 5, 1976) 24.

147ET) "The West and the Truth of Sex." Translated by Lawrence Winters. **Sub-Stance** 20 (1978) 5–8.

148) "Entretien avec Michel Foucault." **Cahiers du Cinéma** 271 (Nov. 1976) 52–53. An interview conducted by Pascal Kane on the Réné Allio film of **Moi, Pierre Rivière**.

149) "Malraux." **Le Nouvel Observateur** 629 (Nov. 29, 1976) 83.

150) "Histoire des systèmes de pensée." **Annuaire du Collège de France** 76 (1976) 361–366. A summary of the course given at the Çollège de France in 1976. Lecture: "'Il faut défendre la societé.'" Seminar: "L'utilisation des techniques psychiatriques en matière pénale."

150ET) "War in the Filigree of Peace. Course Summary." Translated by Ian McLeod. **Oxford Literary Review** IV, 2 (1980) 15–19.

150A) **Vom Licht des Krieges zur Geburt der Geschichte**. Edited by Walter Seitter. Berlin: Merve Verlag, 1986. This volume is made up of German translations of two of the lectures from this course (Jan. 21 and Jan. 28).

151) "Preface." To the English translation of Gilles Deleuze and Felix Guattari, **Anti-Oedipus: Capitalism and Schizophrenia**. Translated by Robert Hurley, Mark Seem and Helen Lane. New York: Viking, 1977, xi-xiv.

152) "Vorwort zu deutschen Ausgabe." An introduction to the German edition of **VS: Sexualität und Wahrheit: I: Die Wille zum Wissen**. Translated by Ulrich Raulf. Frankfurt: Suhrkamp, 1977, 7–8.

153) "Avant-propos." Foreword to **Politiques de l'habitat 1800–1850**, a study done under the direction of MF. Paris: CORDA, 1977, 3–4.

james bernauer
and thomas
keenan

154) "L'oeil du pouvoir." Introduction to Jeremy Betham's **Le panoptique**. Paris: Pierre Belfond, 1977, 7–31. A conversation with Jean-Pierre Barou and Michelle Perrot.

154ET) "The Eye of Power." Translated by Colin Gordon. In **Power/Knowledge**, 146–165.

155) "Le supplice de la vérité." **Chemin de Ronde** 1 (1977) 162–163.

156) "Die Folter, das ist die Vernunft." **Literaturmagazin** 8 (1977) 60–68. A conversation with Kurt Boesers.

157) "Préface." To Mireille Debard and Jean-Luc Hennig, **Les juges kaki**. Paris: Editions Alain Moreau, 1977, 7–10. Also published as "Les juges kaki." **Le Monde** 10214 (Dec. 1–2, 1977) 15.

158) "Historia de la medicalizacion." **Education medica y salud** 11, 1 (1977) 3–25.

159) "Les rapports de pouvoir passent à l'intérieur des corps." An interview conducted by Lucette Finas. **La quinzaine littéraire** 247 (Jan. 1–15, 1977) 4–6.

159ET) "The History of Sexuality." Translated by Leo Marshall. In **Power/Knowledge**, 183–193.

160) "La vie des hommes infâmes." **Les Cahiers du Chemin** 29 (Jan. 15, 1977) 12–29. This piece was to serve as the introduction to a volume to be edited by Foucault and published under the same title by Gallimard.

160ET) "The Life of Infamous Men." Translated by Paul Foss and Meaghan Morris. In the collection of essays they edited, **Power, Truth, Strategy**, (Sydney, Australia: Feral, 1979) 76–91.

161) "Michel Foucault: à bas la dictature du sexe!" **L'Express** 1333 (Jan. 24, 1977) 56–57. A review of **VS** by Madeleine Chapsal, with extensive quotations from an interview with MF.

162) "Pouvoirs et stratégies." **Les révoltes logiques** 4 (Winter, 1977) 89–97.

162ET) "Powers and Strategies." Translated by Colin Gordon. In **Power/Knowledge**, 134–145.

163) "Non au sexe roi." **Le Nouvel Observateur** 644 (March 12, 1977) 92–130. An interview conducted by Bernard-Henri Levy.

163ET) "Power and Sex: An Interview with Michel Foucault." Translated by David Parent. **Telos** 32 (Summer, 1977) 152–161.

164) "Les matins gris de la tolérance." **Le Monde** 9998 (March 23, 1977) 24. A review of a film by P. Pasolini, **Enquête sur la sexualité (Comizi d'Amore)**.

165) "L'asile illimité." **Le Nouvel Observateur** 646 (March 28, 1977) 66–67. A review of Robert Castel's **L'ordre psychiatrique**.

166) "La géometrie de Maxime Defert." **Les Nouvelles Littéraires** 2582 (April 28 1977) 13. Review of an art exhibit.

167) "La grande colère des faits." **Le Nouvel Observateur** 652 (May 9, 1977) 84–86. Reissued in **Faut-il brûler les nouveaux philosophes?**, edited by Sylvie Bouscasse and Denis Bourgeois. Paris: Nouvelles Editions Oswald, 1978, 63–70. A reflection on André Glucksmann's **Les maîtres penseurs**.

168) "L'angoisse de juger." **Le Nouvel Observateur** 655 (May 30, 1977) 92–126. A debate on capital punishment with Robert Badinter and Jean Laplanche, edited by Catherine David.

169) "Le jeu de Michel Foucault." **Ornicar?** 10 (July, 1977) 62- 93. A discussion with MF. Participants were: Alain Grosrichard, Gérard Wajeman, Jacques-Alain Miller, Guy Le Gaufey, Catherine Millot, Dominique Colas, Jocelyne Livi, Judith Miller.

169ET) "The Confession of the Flesh." Translated by Colin Gordon. In **Power/Knowledge**, 194–228.

170) "Une mobilisation culturelle." **Le Nouvel Observateur** 670 (Sept. 12, 1977) 49.

171) "Enfermement, Psychiatrie, Prison." **Change: La folie encerclée** 32–33 (Oct., 1977) 76–110. A dialogue between MF, David Cooper, Victor Fainberg, and Jean-Pierre Faye.

james bernauer
and thomas
keenan

172) "About the Concept of the 'Dangerous Individual' in 19th-Century Legal Psychiatry." Translated by Alain Baudot and Jane Couchman. **International Journal of Law and Psychiatry** I (1978) 1–18. Originally delivered in English at a symposium in Toronto, October 24- 26, 1977.

172A) This was later issued in French as "L'évolution de la notion d''individu dangereux' dans la psychiatrie légale." **Revue déviance et société** V (1981) 403–422.

173) "Va-t-on extrader Kaus Croissant?" **Le Nouvel Observateur** 679 (Nov. 14, 1977) 62–63.

174) "'Désmormais, la sécurité est au-dessus des lois.'" **Le Matin** 225 (Nov. 18, 1977) 15. An interview conducted by Jean-Paul Kauffman.

175) "Lettre à quelques leaders de la gauche." **Le Nouvel Observateur** 681 (Nov. 28, 1977) 59.

176) " 'Wir fühlten uns als schmutzige Spezies.'" **Der Spiegel** 31 (Dec. 19, 1977) 77–78.

177) "Préface." To **My Secret Life**. Translated from the English by Christine Charnaux et al. Paris: Editions les Formes du Secret, 1978, 5–7.

178) "Introduction." To Georges Canguilhem's **On the Normal and the Pathological**. This is the English translation of **Le normal et le pathologique**. Translated by Carolyn Fawcett. Boston: D. Reidel, 1978, ix-xx.

178A) This was later issued in French as "La vie: l'expérience et la science" in **Revue de métaphysique et de morale** 90 (January-March, 1985) 3–14.

179) "Note." To **Herculine Barbin dite Alexina B.** Presented by MF. Paris: Gallimard, 1978, 131–132.

179A) "Introduction." To the English translation: **Herculine Barbin, Being the Recently Discovered Memoirs of a Nineteenth Century French Hermaphrodite**. Translated by Richard McDougall. New York: Pantheon Books, 1980, vii-xvii. This introduction is a totally new work dated January, 1980. The original brief note to the French edition is on pages 119–120 of the translation.

180) "La grille politique traditionelle." **Politique-Hebdo** 303 (1978) 20.

181) "M. Foucault. Conversazione senza complessi con il filosofo che analizza le 'strutture del potere.'" A discussion with J. Bauer. **Playmen** 12, 10 (1978) 21–30.

182) "Incorporacion del hospital en la tecnologia moderna." **Educacion medica y salud** 12, 1 (1978) 20–35.

183) "Un jour dans une classe s'est fait une film." **L'Educateur** 51, 12 (1978) 21–25.

184) "Eugène Sue que j'aime." **Les nouvelle littéraires** 2618 (Jan. 12–19, 1978) 3. A reflection on the reissued **Les mystères du peuple** by Sue.

185) "Une érudition étourdissante." **Le Matin** 278 (January 20, 1978) 25. A review of Philippe Ariès' **L'Homme devant la mort**.

186) "Alain Peyrefitte s'explique . . . et Michel Foucault lui répond." **Le Nouvel Observateur** 689 (Jan. 23, 1978) 25.

187) "Precisazioni sul potere. Riposta ad alcuni critici." **Aut Aut** 167–168 (Sept.-Dec., 1978) 3–11. Response to written questions from Pasquale Pasquino in February, 1978.

188) "La gouvernamentalità." **Aut Aut** 167–168 (Sept.-Dec., 1978) 12–29. The Italian transcript, translated by Pasquale Pasquino, of a lecture given at the Collège de France in February, 1978.

188ET) "Governmentality." Translated by Rosi Braidotti. **Ideology and Consciousness** 6 (Autumn, 1979) 5–21.

188A) This lecture was released in a French translation by Jean-Claude Oswald as "La gouvernementalité," **Actes** 54 (Summer, 1986) 7–15.

189) "Attention: danger." **Libération** 1286 (March 22, 1978) 9.

190) Le poussière et le nuage." **L'impossible prison: Recherches sur le système pénitentiaire au XIXe siècle**. Ed-

james bernauer
and thomas
keenan

ited by Michelle Perrot. Paris: Seuil, 1980, 29–39. Although not published until May, 1980, this was written in 1978 as a reply to a text by Jacques Léonard which appears in the same volume: "L'historien et le philosophe: A propos de: **Surveiller et punir; naissance de la prison**." Both papers served as the basis for a discussion with MF which was published as the following entry.

191) "Table ronde du 20 mai 1978." In **L'impossible prison**, 40–56 (cf. #190 for full details). While specific interventions were not cited by name with the exception of those from MF, participants in this discussion were: Maurice Agulhon, Nicole Caston, Catherine Duprat, Francois Ewald, Arlette Farge, Alexandre Fontana, Carlo Ginzburg, Remi Gossez, Jacques Léonard, Pascal Pasquino, Michelle Perrot, Jacques Revel.

191ET) "Questions of Method." Translated by Colin Gordon. **Ideology and Consciousness** 8 (Spring, 1981) 3–14.

192) "Postface." To **L'impossible prison** (cf. #190), 316–318.

193) "Vijftien vragen van homosexuele zijde san Michel Foucault." **Interviews met Michel Foucault**, ed. by M. Duyves and T. Maasen. Utrecht: De Woelrat, 1982, 13–23.

194) "Du pouvoir." **L'Express** 1722 (July 13, 1984) 56–62. An interview with MF, conducted by Pierre Boncenne in July, 1978 but not published until after Foucault's death.

195) "Du bon usage du criminel." **Le Nouvel Observateur** 722 (Sept. 11, 1978) 40–42.

196) "Taccuino Persiano: L'esercito, quando la terra trema." **Corriere della Sera** 103, No. 228 (Sept. 28, 1978) 1–2. The first of a series of articles in Italian on the revolution in Iran.

197) "Teheran: la fede contro lo Scia." **Corriere della Sera** 103, No. 237 (Oct. 8, 1978) 11.

198) "A quoi rêvent les Iraniens?" **Le Nouvel Observateur** 726 (Oct. 9–16, 1978) 48–49.

199) "Le citron et le lait." **Le Monde** 10, 490 (Oct. 21, 1978) 14. A review of Philippe Boucher's **Le ghetto judiciaire**.

works of
foucault

200) "Ein gewaltiges Erstaunen." An interview on the exposition "Paris-Berlin" which took place in Paris in 1978. **Der Spiegel** 32 (Oct. 30, 1978) 264.

200ET) "Interview with Michel Foucault." Translated by J.D. Steakley. **New German Critique** 16 (Winter, 1979) 155–156.

201) "Une rivolta con le mani nude." **Corriere della Sera**, 103, No. 261 (Nov. 5, 1978) 1–2.

202) "Sfida all'opposizione." **Corriere della Sera**, 103, No. 262 (Nov. 7, 1978) 1–2.

203) "I 'reportages di idee.'" **Corriere della Sera**, 103, No. 267 (Nov. 12, 1978) 1.

204) "Réponse de Michel Foucault à une lectrice iranienne." **Le Nouvel Observateur** 731 (Nov. 13, 1978) 26.

205) "La rivolta dell'Iran corre sui nastri delli minicasette." **Corriere della Sera**, 103 No. 273 (Nov. 19, 1978) 1–2.

206) "Il mitico capo della rivolta nell'Iran." **Corriere della Sera**, 103, No. 279 (Nov. 26, 1978) 1–2.

207) **Colloqui con Foucault**. Salerno: 10/17 Cooperative editrice, 1981. A series of 1978 interviews between MF and Duccio Trombadori.

208) "Lettera di Foucault all'Unita." **L'Unita** 55, no. 285 (December 1, 1978) 1.

209) "Histoire des systèmes de pensée." **Annuaire du Collège de France** 78 (1978) 445–449. A summary of the course given at the Collège de France in 1978. Lecture: "Securité, territoire, et population." Seminar: "La Médicalisation en France depuis le XIXe siècle."

209ET) "Foucault at the Collège de France I: A Course Summary." Translated, with an introduction, by James Bernauer. **Philosophy and Social Criticism** VIII, 2 (Summer, 1981) 235–242.

209A) An edited version of this course's lectures has been translated into German by Andreas Pribersky and published

james bernauer and thomas keenan

as "Vorlesungen zur Analyse der Macht-Mechanismen 1978: Das Denken des Staates." In MF, **Der Staub und die Wolke** (Bremen: Verlag Impuls, 1982) 1–44.

210) "L'esprit d'un monde sans esprit." A conversation with MF conducted by Claire Brière and Pierre Blanchet. Published as an appendix to their **Iran: la révolution au nom de Dieu.** Paris: Seuil, 1979, 225–241.

211) "Préface." To Peter Brückner and Alfred Krovoza, **Ennemi de l'État**. Claix: La pensée sauvage, 1979, 4–5.

212) "La phobie d'etat." **Libération** 967 (June 30-July 1, 1984) 21. An excerpt from a lecture by Foucault on Jan. 31, 1979 at the Collège.

213) "Manières de justice." **Le Nouvel Observateur** 743 (Feb. 5, 1979) 20–21.

214) "Una polveriera chiamata Islam." **Corriere della Sera** 104, No. 36 (Feb. 13, 1979) 1.

215) "Michel Foucault et l'Iran." **Le Matin** 647 (March 26, 1979) 15. A short reply to an article which had attacked his position on Iran's revolution. Cf. Claudie and Jacques Broyelle, "A quoi rêvent les philosophes?" **Le Matin** 646 (March 24, 1979) 13.

216) "La loi de la pudeur." **Recherches** 37 (April, 1979) 69–82. A transcript of radio discussion on April 4, 1978 with Guy Hocquenghem and Jean Danet.

216ET) Excerpts from Foucault's remarks were translated by Daniel Moshenberg and published in **Semiotext(e)** (Summer, 1980) 44, 40- 42.

217) "Une plaisir si simple." **Le Gai Pied** 1 (April, 1979) 1, 10.

217ET) "The Simplest of Pleasures." Translated by Mike Riegle and Gilles Barbedette. **Fag Rag** 29, p. 3.

218) "Lettre ouverte à Mehdi Bazargan." **Le Nouvel Observateur** 753 (April 14, 1979) 46.

219) "Pour une morale de l'inconfort." **Le Nouvel Observateur** 754 (April 23, 1979) 82–83. A review of Jean Daniel's **L'ère des ruptures**.

220) "Le moment de vérité." **Le Matin** 673 (April 25, 1979) 20. On the death of Maurice Clavel.

221) "Vivre autrement le temps." **Le Nouvel Observateur** 755 (April 30, 1979) 88. A testimony to Maurice Clavel.

222) "Inutile de se soulever?" **Le Monde** 10, 661 (May 11, 1979) 1–2.

222ET) "Is it useless to revolt?" Translated, with an introduction, by James Bernauer. **Philosophy and Social Criticism** VIII, 1 (Spring, 1981) 1–9.

223) "La stratégie du pourtour." **Le Nouvel Observateur** 759 (May 28, 1979) 57.

224) "Omnes et Singulatim: Towards a Criticism of 'Political Reason.'" Lectures delivered at Stanford University on Oct. 10 and 16, 1979. In Sterling McMurrin, ed., **The Tanner Lectures on Human Values** II (1981). Salt Lake City: University of Utah Press, 1981, 225–254.

224A) "Omnes et Singulatim: Vers une critique de la raison politique." Translated by P.E. Dauzat. **Le débat** 41 (Sept.-Nov., 1986) 5- 35.

225) "Luttes autour des prisons." **Esprit** 35 (Nov., 1979) 102-111. A discussion between MF (under the pseudonym of "Louis Appert"), Anotoine Lazarus, and Francois Colcombet, on the prison movements of the 1970s.

226) "Histoire des systèmes de pensée." **Annuaire du Collège de France** 79 (1979) 367–372. A summary of the course given at the Collège de France, in 1979. Lecture: "Naissance de la biopolitique." Seminar: "Problèmes de méthode en histoire des idées."

226ET) "Foucault at the Collège de France II: A Course Summary." Translated, with an introduction, by James Bernauer. **Philosophy and Social Criticism** VIII, 3 (Fall, 1981) 349–359.

227) "Les quatre cavaliers de l'Apocalypse." **Cahiers du cinéma** 6 (1980) 95–96.

228) " 'Le Nouvel Observateur' e l'unione della sinistre." **Spirali** 15 (Jan., 1980) 53–55. Excerpts from a conversation between MF and Jean Daniel, first broadcast on a France-Culture radio program conducted by Denis Richet.

229) "Lettre." **Le Nouvel Observateur** (Jan. 14, 1980).

230) "Préface." To Roger Knobelspiess, **Q.H.S.: Quartier de haute sécurité**. Paris: Stock, 1980, 11–16 (March 31, 1980).

231) "Le philosophe masqué." **Le Monde Dimanche** 10,945 (April 6, 1980) I and XVII. An interview conducted by Christian Delacampagne and originally published without identifying Foucault.

232) "Conversation with Michel Foucault." **The Threepenny Review** I, 1 (Winter-Spring,1980) 4–5. An interview conducted by Millicent Dillon.

233) "Sexuality and Solitude." **London Review of Books** (May 21- June 3, 1981) 3, 5–6. The text of Foucault's James Lecture, delivered Nov. 20, 1980 at the New York Institute for the Humanities. This was later published in **Humanities in Review** I (1982), edited by David Rieff. New York: Cambridge University Press, 1982, 3–21.

234) "Le vrai sexe." **Arcadie** 27 (November, 1980) 617–625.

235) "Roland Barthes." **Annuaire du Collège de France** 80 (1980) 61–62.

236) "Histoire des systèmes de pensée." **Annuaire du Collège de France** 80 (1980) 449–452. A summary of the course given at the Collège de France in 1980. Lecture: "Du gouvernement des vivants." Seminar: "Liberalisme et Etatisme à la fin du fin du XIXe siècle."

237) "De l'amitié comme mode de vie." **Le Gai Pied** 25 (April, 1981) 38–39.

237ET) "Friendship as a Lifestyle: An Interview with Michel Foucault." **Gay Information** 7 (Spring, 1981) 4–6. No translator identified.

238) "L'intellectuel et les pouvoirs." **La Revue Nouvelle** 80 (1984) 338–345. Interview conducted on May 14, 1981 by Christian Panier and Pierre Watté.

239) "Est-il donc important de penser?" **Libération** (May 30-31, 1981) 21. An interview with MF conducted by Didier Eribon.

239ET) "Is it really important to think?" Translated, with an afterword, by Thomas Keenan. **Philosophy and Social Criticism** 9, 1 (Spring 1982) 29–40.

240) "Face aux gouvernements, les droits de l'Homme." **Libération** 967 (June 30-July 1, 1984) 22. A statement by Foucault in June, 1981, but published only after his death. It concerned Southeast Asian "boat people."

241) "Il faut tout repenser la loi et la prison." **Libération** 45 (July 6, 1981) 2. On hunger strikes by prison inmates.

242) "Lacan, il 'liberatore' della psicanalisi." **Corriere della Sera** 106, No. 212 (Sept. 11, 1981) 1. An interview with MF conducted by Jacques Nobécourt after the death of Jacques Lacan.

243) "De la nécessité de mettre un terme à toute peine." **Libération** 108 (Sept. 18, 1981) 5.

244) "Les réponses de Pierre Vidal-Naquet et de Michel Foucault." **Libération** 185 (Dec. 18, 1981) 12. Concerns the French governments's reaction to the imposition of martial law in Poland.

245) "Conversation." In Gérard Courant (ed.), **Werner Schroeter.** Paris: Cinématheque Francaise et Goethe Institute, 1982, 38–47. A discussion between MF and Werner Schroeter as recorded by Courant on December 3, 1981.

246) "Notes sur ce qu'on lit et entend." **Le Nouvel Observateur** 893 (Dec. 19, 1981) 21. On the imposition of martial law in Poland.

247) "Histoire des systèmes de pensée." **Annuaire du Collège de France** 81 (1981) 385–389. A summary of the course given at the Collège de France in 1981. Lecture: "Subjectivité

et vérité." Seminar: "Problèmes du liberalisme au XIXe siècle."

248) **Le désordre des familles: Lettres de cachet des Ar-
chives de la Bastille**. A collection of police documents, edited
with introductions by MF and Arlette Farge. Paris: Gallimard/
Julliard, 1982.

249) "Nineteenth Century Imaginations." Translated by Alex
Susteric. **Semiotext(e)** IV, 2 (1982)182–190.

250) "The Subject and Power." An afterword to Hubert Drey-
fus and Paul Rabinow, **Michel Foucault: Beyond Structur-
alism and Hermeneutics**. Chicago: University of Chicago
Press, 1982, 214–32. Part I was written in English by Foucault;
Part II was translated by Leslie Sawyer. Republished in **Critical
Inquiry** 8 (Summer, 1982).

251) "Non aux compromis." **Gai Pied** 43 (1982) 9. A conversation with R. Surzur.

252) Response to speech by Susan Sontag. **The Soho News**
(March 2, 1982) 13.

253) "Space, Knowledge, and Power." **Skyline** (March, 1982)
16–20. An interview with P. Rabinow, translated by Christian
Hubert.

254) "Histoire et Homosexualité: Entretien avec M. Foucault."
Masques 13 (Spring, 1982) 14–24. An interview conducted
by J.P. Joecker, M. Ouerd and A. Sanzio.

255) "Sexual Choice, Sexual Act: An Interview with Michel
Foucault." **Salmagundi** 58–59 (Fall, 1982-Winter, 1983) 10–
24. Conducted by James O'Higgins in March 1982.

255A) This appeared in French as "Lorsque l'amant part en
taxi." **Gai Pied Hebdo** 151 (January 5, 1985) 22–24, 54–57.

256) "La combat de la chasteté." **Communications** 35 (May,
1982) 15–25.

256ET) "The Battle for Chastity." In **Western Sexuality: Practice and Precept in Past and Present Times**, edited by Phil-

149

ippe Ariès and André Béjin and translated by Anthony Foster. Oxford: Basil Blackwell, 1985, 14–25.

257) "The Social Triumph of the Sexual Will." **Christopher Street** 64 (May, 1982) 36–41. A conversation with MF, conducted by Gilles Barbedette and translated by Brendan Lemon.

258) "Des caresses d'homme considérées comme un art." **Libération** (June 1, 1982) 27. A review of K.J. Dover's **Homosexualité grecque**.

259) "An Interview." **Ethos** I, 2 (Autumn, 1983) 4–9. Conducted by Stephen Riggins on June 22, 1982.

260) "Michel Foucault, An Interview: Sex, Power and the Politics of Identity," **The Advocate** 400 (Aug. 7, 1984) 26–30, 58. Conducted by Bob Gallagher and Alexander Wilson in June, 1982.

260A) This later appeared in a French translation by Jacques Hess as "Que fabriquent donc les hommes ensemble?" **Le Nouvel Observateur** 1098 (Nov. 22–28, 1985) 54–55.

261) "Le terrorisme ici et la." **Libération** (Sept. 3, 1982) 12. A discussion with D. Eribon.

262) "Pierre Boulez ou l'écran traversé." **Le Nouvel Observateur** 934 (Oct. 2, 1982) 51–52.

263) "En abandonnant les Polonais, nous renoncons à une part de nous-mêmes." **Le Nouvel Observateur** 935 (Oct. 9, 1982) 36. A conversation with Bernard Kouchner and Simone Signoret, conducted by Pierre Blanchet.

264) "L'expérience morale et sociale des Polonais ne peut plus être effacée." **Les nouvelles littéraires** 2857 (Oct. 14–20, 1982) 8–9. An interview with MF conducted by Gilles Anquetil.

265) "La Pensée, L'Emotion." In **Duane Michals: Photographies de 1958 à 1982**. Paris: Paris Audiovisual, Musée d'Art Moderne de la Ville de Paris, 1982, iii-vii. An exposition at the Musée d'Art Moderne in Paris, Nov. 9, 1982-Jan. 9, 1983.

150

james bernauer
and thomas
keenan

266) "L'âge d'or de la lettre de cachet." **L'Express** 1638 (Dec. 3, 1982) 35–36. An interview with MF and Arlette Farge, conducted by Yves Hersant on **Le Désordre des familles** (#248 above).

267) "Histoire des systèmes de pensée." **Annuaire du Collège de France** 82 (1982) 395–406. A summary of the course given at the Collège de France in 1982. Lecture: "L'hermeneutique du sujet." An abridged presentation of Foucault's lectures was edited and published by Helmut Becker and Lothar Wolfstetter as "Michel Foucaults Hermeneutik des Subjekts" in their collection **Freiheit und Selbstsorge** (Frankfurt: Materialis Verlag, 1985) 32–60.

268) "L'écriture de soi." **Corps écrit** 5 (1983): **L'autoportrait**, 3–23.

269) "Rêver de ses plaisirs: sur l'onirocritique d'Artémidore." **Recherches sur la philosophie et le langage** 3 (1983) 53–78. A slightly altered version of this material became chapter 1 of **Le souci de soi**. Cf. #286 below.

270) "Un système fini face à une demande infinie." In **Sécurité sociale: l'enjeu**. Paris: Editions Syros, 1983, 39–63. An interview with R. Bono.

270ET) "The Risks of Security." **History of the Present** 2 (Spring, 1986) 4–5, 11–14.

271) "Un cours inédit." **Magazine littéraire** 207 (May, 1984) 35–39. A lecture at the Collège de France, January 5, 1983, on the question of enlightenment in Kant.

271ET) "Kant on Enlightenment and Revolution." Translated by Colin Gordon. **Economy and Society** 15 (February, 1986) 88–96.

272) "À propos des faiseurs d'histoire." **Libération** (Jan. 21, 1983) 22. An interview with Didier Eribon.

273) "An Exchange with Michel Foucault." An exchange of letters between MF and Lawrence Stone. **The New York Review of Books** (March 31, 1983) 42–44. Foucault's letter was written in criticism of Stone's earlier essay, "Madness," in **The New York Review of Books** (Dec. 16, 1982) 28–36.

274) "Structuralism and Post-Structuralism: An Interview with Michel Foucault." **Telos** 55 (Spring, 1983) 195–211. An interview conducted by Gérard Raulet and translated by Jeremy Harding. First published in German as "Um welchen Preis sagt die Vernunft die Wahrheit?" **Spuren** 1–2 (1983).

275) "The Power and Politics of Michel Foucault." **Inside** (April 22, 1983) 7, 20–22. An interview in the weekly magazine of the **Daily Californian** (University of California at Berkeley) conducted by Peter Maass and David Brock.

276) "Politics and Ethics: An Interview." Translated by Catherine Porter. In **The Foucault Reader**, edited by Paul Rabinow (New York: Pantheon Books, 1984) 373–380. Edited interviews conducted in April, 1983, by Paul Rabinow, Charles Taylor, Martin Jay, Richard Rorty and Leo Lowenthal.

277) "On the Genealogy of Ethics: An Overview of Work in Progress." In the 2nd edition of their **Michel Foucault: Beyond Structuralism and Hermeneutics**. Chicago: University of Chicago Press, 1983, 229–252. An interview conducted by Hubert Dreyfus and Paul Rabinow. An abridged French translation by Jacques B. Hess appeared as "Le sexe comme une morale." **Le Nouvel Observateur** (June 1, 1984) 62–66.

278) "La Pologne, et après? Edmond Maire: Entretien avec Michel Foucault." **Le débat** 25 (May, 1983) 3–34.

279) "La Musique contemporaine et le publique." **CNAC Magazine** 15 (May-June, 1983) 10–12. A discussion between MF and Pierre Boulez, in the magazine of the Pompidou Center.

280) "Vous êtes dangereux." **Libération** 639 (June 10, 1983) 20.

281) "Archéologie d'une passion." **Magazine littéraire** 221 (July-August, 1985) 100–105. An edited interview conducted by Charles Ruas on Sept. 15, 1983.

281ET) "An Interview with Michel Foucault." Postscript to Ruas's translation of **Raymond Roussel** (cf. #18 above), 169–186.

282) "Usage des plaisirs et techniques de soi." **Le débat** 27 (November, 1983) 46–72. This is a very slightly modified ver-

sion of the introductory chapter to **L'usage des plaisirs**. Cf. #285 below.

283) "Qu'appelle-t-on punir?" **Revue de l'université de Bruxelles** (1984): **Punir mon bon souci, Pour une raison penale**, 35–46. An interview with Foulek Ringelheim, conducted in December 1983.

284) "Histoire des systèmes de pensée." **Annuaire du Collège de France** 83 (1983) 441. Foucault's last submitted course description reads simply: Le cours a porté sur: "Le gouvernement de soi et des autres."

285) **Histoire de la sexualité 2: L'usage des plaisirs**. Paris: Gallimard, 1984.

285ET) **The Use of Pleasure**. Translated by Robert Hurley. New York: Pantheon, 1985.

285A) Earlier version of "Preface." Translated by William Smock. In **The Foucault Reader**, 333–339.

286) **Histoire de la sexualité 3: Le souci de soi**. Paris: Gallimard, 1984.

286ET) **The Care of the Self**. Translated by Robert Hurley. New York: Pantheon, 1986.

287) "Interview met Michel Foucault." **Krisis: Tijdschrift voor filosofie** 14 (1984) 47–58. A discussion with J. Francois and J. de Wit.

288) "L'éthique du souci de soi comme pratique de liberté." **Concordia** 6 (1984) 99–116. An interview with Raul Fornet-Betancourt, Helmut Becker and Alfredo Gomez-Müller, conducted on Jan. 20, 1984.

288ET) "The Ethics of Care of the Self as a Practice of Freedom." Translated by Joseph Gauthier. **Philosophy and Social Criticism** XII, 2–3, 112–131.

289) "Philippe Ariès: Le souci de la vérité." **Le Nouvel Observateur** 1006 (Feb. 17–23, 1984) 56–57.

290) "Le style de l'histoire." **Le Matin** 2168 (Feb. 21, 1984) 20–21. Interview conducted by Francois Dumont and Jean-Paul Iommi-Amunstegui, with Arlette Farge, on Philippe Ariès.

153 291) "A Last Interview with French Philosopher Michel Foucault." **City Paper** 8, 30 (July 27-Aug. 2, 1984) 18. Conducted by Jamin Raskin in March, 1984.

292) "Interview de Michel Foucault." **Actes** 45–46 (1984): **La prison autrement?**, 3–6. An interview conducted by Catherine Baker in April, 1984.

293) "Le souci de la vérité." **Magazine littéraire** 207 (May, 1984) 18–23. An interview conducted by Francois Ewald.

293ET) "The Regard for Truth." An abridged translation, with an introduction, by Paul Patton. **Art and Text** 16 (Summer, 1984) 20–31.

294) "What Is Enlightenment?" A translation by Catherine Porter of an unpublished French text. In **The Foucault Reader**, 31–50.

295) "Une esthétique de l'existence." **Le Monde Aujourd'hui** (July 15–16, 1984) xi. An interview with Alessandro Fontana on April 25, 1984.

296) "Polemics, Politics and Problematizations." Translated by Lydia Davis. In **The Foucault Reader**, 381–389. Foucault's written responses to questions from Paul Rabinow and Tom Zummer in May, 1984, based on the transcript of an interview conducted earlier.

297) "Pour en finir avec les mensonges." **Le Nouvel Observateur** 1076 (June 21–27, 1985) 76–77. An interview conducted by Didier Eribon.

298) "Le retour de la morale." **Les Nouvelles** 2937 (June 28-July 5, 1984) 36–41. An interview conducted by Gilles Barbedette and André Scala. Conducted on May 29, 1984, this is probably the last interview which Foucault gave.

298ET) "Final Interview." Translated by Thomas Levin and Isabelle Lorenz. **Raritan** V, 1 (Summer, 1985) 1–13.

B) Miscellaneous Materials

1) Excerpt from an April, 1968 letter from MF to Maurice Clavel. Published in Clavel's **Ce que je crois** (Paris: Grasset, 1975) 138–139.

james bernauer
and thomas
keenan

2) "Création d'un 'Groupe d'Information sur les prisons.'" **Esprit** 401 (March, 1971) 531–532. Co-signed by MF, Jean-Marie Domenach, and Pierre Vidal-Naquet.

3) "Ceremonie, Théatre, et Politique au XVIIe Siècle." **Acta 1. Proceedings of the Fourth Annual Conference of XVIIth Century French Literature**. Minneapolis: University of Minnesota Graduate School, 1972, 22–23. A summary in English by Stephen Davidson of a lecture given at the University on April 7, 1972.

4) "Power and Norm: Notes." Notes from a lecture at the Collège de France on March 28, 1973. Translated by W. Suchting, in **Power, Truth, Strategy**, 59–66.

5) A radio interview of an hour between MF and Jacques Chancel, "Radioscopie," on March 10, 1975. A tape of this interview is available at the library of the Georges Pompidou Center in Paris.

6) "Punir ou guérir." Dialogues, Radio-France (Oct. 8, 1976).

7) Toujours les prisons." An exchange of letters with Paul Thibaud and Jean-Marie Domenach in **Esprit** 37 (January, 1980) 184–186.

8) Otto Friedrich. "France's Philosopher of Power." **Time** 118, No. 20 (Nov. 6, 1981) 147–148. A news article with extensive quotations from an interview with MF.

9) **Discourse and Truth: The Problematization of Parrhesia**. Notes to the Fall, 1983 seminar given by MF at the University of California, Berkeley. A privately printed transcription of Foucault's presentations by Joseph Pearson.

10) A July, 1983 letter to Hervé Guibert. In "L'autre journal d'Hervé Guibert." **L'Autre Journal** 10 (December, 1985) 5.

11) Letters of and conversations with MF quoted extensively in Claude Mauriac's series "Les Temps immobile," published by Grasset in Paris: vol. 2, **Les Espaces imaginaires** (1975); vol. 3, **Et comme l'espérance est violente** (1976); vol. 7, **Signes, rencontres, et rendez-vous** (1983); vol. 9, **Mauriac et fils** (1986); and in **Une Certain rage**. Paris: Laffont, 1977.

C) Studies conducted under the direction of MF

1) **Moi Pierre Rivière, ayant égorgé ma mère, ma soeur et mon frère**. Paris: Gallimard, 1973. A study done under Foucault's direction at the Collège de France. For his own contributions to this volume, cf. the preceding section of the bib-

liography, #99 and 100. The other contents of the study are listed here. The English translations were done by Frank Jellinek and published as: **I, Pierre Riviere, having slaughtered my mother, my sister and my brother** (New York: Pantheon, 1975).

I: "Le dossier" of the parricide, Pierre Rivière.

ET) "The Dossier." This translation omits several passages from the Dossier as well as several documents included in the original.

A) Rivière's memoir was made into a movie by René Allio and released under the same title in 1976 (Paris: Planfilm). Its screenplay is available in **Cinéma** 183 (1977).

II: Notes

1) "L'animal, le fou, le mort," by J.P. Peter and Jeanne Favret.

ET) "The Animal, the Madman and Death."

2) "Les circonstances atténuantes," by Patricia Moulin.

ET) "Extenuating Circumstances."

3) "Regicide-parricide," by Blandine Barret-Kriegel.

ET) "Regicide and Parricide."

4) "Les vies parallèles de P. Rivière," by Ph. Riot.

ET) "The Parallel Lives of Pierre Rivière."

5) "Les médecins et les juges," by Robert Castel.

ET) "The Doctors and the Judges."

6) "Les intermittences de la raison," by Alexandre Fontana.

ET) "The Intermittences of Rationality."

2) Généalogie des équipements de normalisation: les équipements sanitaires. Fontenay-sous-Bois: Centre d'études, de recherches et de formation institutionnelles (CERFI), 1976. Although the entire volume was identified as under Foucault's direction, it seems that he was actually involved only with Part I: "L'institution hospitalière au XVIIIe siècle." The members of the group he directed are unidentified. For Foucault's introduction to the study, cf. the preceding section of the bibliography, #136. The study's list of contents is as follows:

La politique de la santé au XVIIIe siècle

james bernauer
and thomas
keenan

3) Politiques de l'habitat 1800–1850. Paris: Comité pour la Recherche et le Développement en Architecture (CORDA), 1977. For Foucault's brief introduction, cf. the first section of the bibliography, #153. The following studies make up the volume.

1) "Reflexions sur la notion d'habitat aux XVIIIe et XIXe siè-cles," by Ann Thalamy.

2) "Les demeures de la misère. Le choléra-morbus et l'émer-gence de l'"Habitat,'" by Blandine Barret-Kriegel.

3) "Anatomie des discours de réforme," by Jean-Marie Al-liaume.

4) "'La loi du 13 juillet 1850 sur le logements insalubres.' Les philanthropes et le problème insoluble de l'Habitat du pauvre," by Danielle Rancière.

5) "Savoirs de la ville et de la maison au début du XIXe siècle," by Francois Béguin.

michel foucault: a biographical chronology[1]

1926

Born on October 15th in Poitiers.

Secondary studies in Poitiers at the Lycée de Poitiers and at the Jesuit Collège St. Stanislas.

What strikes me now when I try to recall those impressions is that nearly all the great emotional memories I have are related to the political situation. I remember very well that I experienced one of my first great frights when Chancellor Dollfuss was assassinated by the Nazis in, I think, 1934. It is something very far from us now. Very few people remember the murder of Dollfuss. I remember very well that I was really scared by that. I think it was my first strong fright about death. I also remember refugees from Spain arriving in Poitiers. I remember fighting in school with my classmates about the Ethiopian War. I think boys and girls of this generation had their childhood formed by these great historical events. The menace of war was our background, our framework of existence. Then the war arrived. Much more than the activities of family life, it was these events concerning the world which are the substance of our memory. I say "our" because I am nearly sure that most boys and girls in France at this moment had the same experience. Our private life was really threatened. Maybe that is the reason why I am fascinated by history and the relationship between personal experience and those events of which we are a part.[2]

1945

Held the post of Khâgne at the Lycée Henri IV in Paris where Jean Hyppolite taught him philosophy for several months.

1946

Beginning of studies at the École normale supérieure.

1948

Licence de philosophie.

1949

Licence de psychologie.

1951

Agrégation de philosophie.

1952

Diplôme de psycho-pathologie from the Institut de psychologie of Paris.[3]

I was studying psychology in the Hôpital Ste. Anne. It was the early '50s. There was no clear professional status for psychologists in a mental hospital. So as a student in psychology (I studied first philosophy and then psychology) I had a very strange status there. The 'chef de service' was very kind to me and let me do anything I wanted. But nobody worried about what I should be doing. I was free to do anything. I was actually in a position between the staff and the patients, and it wasn't my merit, it wasn't because I had a special attitude, it was the consequence of this ambiguity in my status which forced me to maintain a distance from the staff. I am sure it was not my personal merit because I felt all that at the time as a kind of malaise. It was only a few years later when I started writing a book on the history of psychiatry that this malaise, this personal experience, took the form of an historical criticism or a structural analysis.[4]

Assistant in the Faculty of Letters at the University of Lille.

1955–58

Assistant at the University of Uppsala.[5]

Anyway, I have suffered and I still suffer from a lot of things in French social and cultural life. That was the reason why I left France in 1955. Incidentally, in 1966 and 1968 I also spent two years in Tunisia for purely personal reasons . . . At the moment when I left France, freedom for personal life was very sharply restricted there. At this time Sweden was supposed to be a much freer country. And there I had the experience that a certain kind of freedom may have, not exactly the same effects, but as many restrictive effects as a directly restrictive society. That was an important experience for me.[6]

160

1958

Director of the French Center at the University of Warsaw.[7]

Then I had the opportunity of spending one year in Poland, where, of course, the restrictions and oppressive power of the Communist party are really something quite different. In a rather short period of time I had the experience of an old traditional society, as France was in the late 1940s and early 1950s, and the new free society which was Sweden. I won't say I had the total experience of all the political possibilities but I had a sample of what the possibilities of Western societies were at that moment. That was a good experience.[8]

Accepting that he had a view that was not complete

1959

Director of the French Institute in Hamburg.

1960

Maître de conférences in psychology in the Faculty of Letters at the University of Clermont-Ferrand.

1961

Thèse de doctorat ès lettres: **Histoire de la folie à l'âge classique**.

Thèse complémentaire: An introduction to and translation into French of Kant's **Anthropologie du point de vue pragmatique**.

Danger of Science so-called expertise

*When I was studying during the early 1950s, one of the great problems that arose was that of the political status of science and the ideological functions which it would serve. It wasn't exactly the Lysenko business which dominated everything, but I believe that around that sordid affair—which had long remained buried and carefully hidden—a whole number of interesting questions were provoked. These can all be summed up in two words: power and knowledge. I believe I wrote **Madness and Civilization** to some extent within the horizon of these questions. For me, it was a matter of saying this: if, concerning a science like theoretical physics or organic chemistry, one poses the problem of its relations with the political and economic structures of society, isn't one posing an excessively complicated question? Doesn't this set the threshold of possible explanations impossibly high? But on the other hand, if one takes a form of knowledge (**savoir**) like psychiatry, won't the question be much easier to resolve, since the epistemological profile of psychiatry is a low one and psychiatric practice is linked with a whole range of institutions, economic requirements and political issues of social regulation? Couldn't the interweaving of effects of power and knowledge be grasped*

161

*Dubious
nature o
psychiatry*

*with greater certainty in the case of a science as 'dubious' as
psychiatry? It was this same question which I wanted to pose
concerning medicine in* **The Birth of the Clinic**: *medicine cer-
tainly has a much more solid scientific armature than psychiatry, but it too is profoundly enmeshed in social structures.
What rather threw me at the time was the fact that the question
I was posing totally failed to interest those to whom I addressed it. They regarded it as a problem which was politically
unimportant and epistemologically vulgar.*[9]

1962

Promoted to Professor of Philosophy at the University of Clermont-Ferrand.

1965

In Brazil when the military government was installed. It was
the beginning of a long relationship with the democratic opposition.

1966

In Tunisia.

1967

In June, Foucault was chosen to become Professor of Philosophy at Nanterre. When the Minister of Education delayed his
ratification of the choice, Foucault returned to Tunisia, where
he prepared a never published work on Manet, **Le Noir et la
Couleur**.

1968

Foucault returns to France and participates in the establishment of the experimental university at Vincennes. He is in
charge of the Philosophy Department.

*I think that before '68, at least in France, you had to be as a
philosopher a Marxist, or a phenomenologist, or a structuralist,
and I adhered to none of these dogmas. The second point is
that at this time in France studying psychiatry or the history
of medicine had no real status in the political field. Nobody
was interested in that. The first thing that happened after '68
was that Marxism as a dogmatic framework declined and new
political, new cultural interests concerning personal life appeared. That's why I think my work had nearly no echo with
the exception of a very small circle, before '68.*[10]

*this our
power impacts.*

1969

Elected to the Collège de France where he names his Chair
the "History of Systems of Thought."

1970

December 2nd: Foucault's Inaugural Lecture at the Collège, "The Discourse on Language."

First lectures in the United States and Japan.

1971

Creation of the Groupe information sur les prisons.

Foucault's course at the Collège initiates a series of analyses of the will to knowledge.

1972

At the Collège, Foucault's lectures began an analysis of the social controls and systems of punishment which were characteristic of nineteenth century France.

Visit to Attica Prison, New York State.

*At Attica, what struck me perhaps first of all was the entrance, that kind of phony fortress à la Disneyland, those observation posts disguised as medieval towers with their **machicoulis**. And behind this rather ridiculous scenery which dwarfs everything else, you discover it's an immense machine. And it's this notion of machinery that struck me most strongly—those very long, clean, heated corridors which prescribe, for those who pass through them, specific trajectories that are evidently calculated to be the most efficient possible and at the same time the easiest to oversee, and the most direct.*

A problem has arisen for me which is rather different from ones that I had been puzzling over formerly; the change was perhaps not absolutely determined by the visit to Attica, but the visit surely precipitated it. Until then I envisioned exclusion from society as a sort of general function, a bit abstract, and I tried to plot that function as in some way constitutive of society, each society being able to function only on condition that a certain number of people are excluded from it. Traditional sociology, sociology of the Durheim type presented the problem rather in this way: How can society hold individuals together? What is the form of relationship, of symbolic or affective communication that is established among individuals? What is the totality? I was interested by the somewhat opposite problem, or, if you will, by the opposite response to this problem, which is: Through what system of exclusion, by eliminating whom, by creating what division, through what game of negation and rejection can society begin to function?

Well, the question that I ask myself now is the reverse: <u>prison</u> is an organization that is too complex to be reduced to purely

163

[handwritten margin note: use of exclusion to form society]

*negative functions of exclusion; its cost, its importance, the
care that one takes in administering it, the justifications that
one tries to give it seem to indicate that it possesses positive
functions.*[11]

1973

Foucault's course at the Collège examined the developments
which led up to the birth of the prison.

1974

Foucault's teaching returned to a study of madness and the
institution of confinement but within the context of a disciplinary society and of the different movements which emerge
within it as a critique of psychiatry.

1975

Foucault's course at the Collège studied the constitution of
groups considered to be abnormal.

1976

In his lectures at the Collège, Foucault studied the appearance
of a discourse on war and how it functioned as an analysis of
history and of social relations.

1978

Foucault reports on the Iranian Revolution for the Italian news-
paper **Corriere della Sera**.

Visit to Japan, where he lectures on pastoral power. He studies
Zen as well as Christian and Buddhist mysticism.

Foucault's course treated the genesis of a political knowledge
which places the notion of population and the mechanisms to
assure its regulation at the center of concern.

1979

With a specific consideration of western liberalism, Foucault's
teaching dwelt on the issue of bio-politics.

1980

Foucault's course at the Collège examines the Christian experience of sexuality and its technology of the self.

1981

Foucault begins a collaboration with the democratic Polish
labor union Solidarity. At the Collège, Foucault examines the
formation of the relationship between truth and subjectivity in
Greek culture.

1982

Foucault's course examines the formation of a hermeneutics of the self in ancient Greek and Roman practices.

1983

Foucault's teaching concentrates on the theme of the governance of the self and of truth-telling (parrhesia) as a political virtue.

1984

The theme of Foucault's teaching at the Collège was the Greek practice of truth-telling as a moral virtue.

The publication of his last works, **The Use of Pleasure** and **The Care of the Self**.

*A theoretical shift had seemed necessary in order to analyze what was often designated as the advancement of learning; it led me to examine the forms of discursive practices that articulated the human sciences. A theoretical shift had also been required in order to analyze what is often described as the manifestations of "power"; it led me to examine, rather, the manifold relations, the open strategies, and the rational techniques that articulate the exercise of powers. It appeared that I now had to undertake a third shift, in order to analyze what is termed "the subject." It seemed appropriate to look for the forms and modalities of the relation to self by which the individual constitutes and recognizes himself qua subject. After first studying the games of truth (**jeux de vérité**) in their interplay with one another, as exemplified by certain empirical sciences in the seventeenth and eighteenth centuries, and then studying their interaction with power relations, as exemplified by punitive practices—I felt obliged to study the games of truth in the relationship of self with self and the forming of oneself as a subject, taking as my domain of reference and field of investigation what might be called "the history of desiring man."*[12]

June 25th, Michel Foucault dies in Paris.

NOTES

1. This chronology is dependent upon Daniel Defert's notes, "Quelques repères chronologiques," in **Michel Foucault: Une histoire de la vérité** (Paris: Syros, 1985) pp. 109–114. My choice of remarks from Foucault is governed by biographical interest as well as by the emergence of the three distinct axes of his work: knowledge—power—subjectivity. (JB)

2. "Michel Foucault: An Interview," conducted by Stephen Riggins on June 22, 1982, in **Ethos** I, 2 (Autumn, 1983) p.5.

3. For a remembrance of Foucault as a student and young writer, cf. Maurice Pinguet, "Les années d'apprentissage," **Le débat** 41 (Sept.-Nov., 1986) pp.122–131.

4. "Michel Foucault: An Interview" (Riggins), p.5.

5. For a remembrance of Foucault during his years in Sweden, cf. Jean Piel, "Foucault à Uppsala," **Critique** 471–472 (Aug.-Sept., 1986) pp.748–752.

6. "Michel Foucault: An Interview" (Riggins), p.4.

7. For a recollection of Foucault at this time, cf. the article by the former French Ambassador to Poland, Étienne Burin des Roziers, "Une rencontre à Varsovie," **Le débat** 41 (Sept.-Nov., 1986) pp.132–136.

8. "Michel Foucault: An Interview" (Riggins), p.4.

9. "Truth and Power," an interview with Michel Foucault conducted by A. Fontana and P. Pasquino in **Power/Knowledge: Selected Interviews and Other Writings** 1972–1977, edited by Colin Gordon (New York: Pantheon, 1980) pp.109–110.

10. "Michel Foucault: An Interview" (Riggins), p.4.

11. "Michel Foucault on Attica," an interview with John Simon in 1972, **Telos** 19 (1974) 155–156.

12. **The Use of Pleasure**, trans. by Robert Hurley (New York: Pantheon, 1985) p.6.

Notes on Contributors

James Bernauer, Associate Professor of Philosophy at Boston College, is the editor of **Amor Mundi: Explorations in the Faith and Thought of Hannah Arendt** (Martinus Nijhoff, 1987). He received his doctorate in philosophy from the State University of New York at Stony Brook, and attended Foucault's 1979 and 1980 courses at the Collège de France.

Thomas R. Flynn, Ph.D. Columbia, is the author of **Sartre and Marxist Existentialism. The Test Case of Collective Responsibility** (University of Chicago Press, 1984; pbk. 1986) as well as numerous articles on Sartre, Foucault and other topics. He is Associate Professor of Philosophy at Emory University and currently serves on the Executive Board of the Society for Phenomenology and Existential Philosophy. He attended Foucault's last lectures in Paris under a senior research grant from the American Council of Learned Societies.

Joseph Gauthier, Professor of Romance Languages at Boston College, has his Doctorat ès Lettres from Laval University. His many writings include studies of Mauriac, Malraux, Gide and Sartre.

Garth Jackson Gillan received his doctorate from Duquesne University and is currently teaching at Southern Illinois University, Carbondale, Illinois in the department of philosophy. He has edited a volume of essays on Merleau-Ponty and published two other works: **From Sign to Symbol** (Harvester) and, with Charles Lemert, **Michel Foucault: Social Theory as Trangression** (Columbia University Press). He is presently at work on a book on the epistemology of symbols.

Thomas Keenan is a Ph.D. candidate in Comparative Literature at Yale University. He has translated and written on Foucault. He is now finishing a dissertation entitled "Fables of Responsibility: Politics between Literature and Philosophy," as well as editing a collection of Jacques Derrida's political writings.

Karlis Racevskis is the author of **Voltaire and the French Academy** (1975), of **Michel Foucault and the Subversion of Intellect** (1983), and has published articles on the Enlightenment, the New Novel, and the Structuralist period. He is Professor of French at Wright State University and is currently writing on recent developments in French cultural criticism.

David M. Rasmussen received his doctorate from the University of Chicago in 1968. He is editor-in-chief of **Philosophy and Social Criticism**. He is author of **Mythic-Symbolic Language and Philosophical Anthropology**, Nijhoff 1971 and **Symbol and Interpretation**, Nijhoff 1974. He is author of numerous articles in social and political philosophy. Currently, he is writing a book on the thought of Jürgen Habermas.

Diane Rubenstein is an Assistant Professor of Political Science at the University of Wisconsin. She received her Ph.D. degree from Yale in 1985. She is the author of a volume on the Ecole Normale Supérieure and the Right. She is currently at work on a book concerning the institution of philosophy in France.

The editors acknowledge with special thanks Deanne Harper for her work in preparing this volume.